READINGS ON EQUAL EDUCATION
(Formerly *Educating the Disadvantaged*)

READINGS
ON EQUAL
EDUCATION

Volume 12

CIVIL RIGHTS

IN SCHOOLS

Edited by

Steven S. Goldberg

with

Kathleen Kelley Lynch

AMS PRESS
NEW YORK

Copyright © 1995 by AMS Press, Inc.
All rights reserved.

Library of Congress Catalogue Number: 77-83137
International Standard Book Number: Set 0-404-10100-3
International Standard Book Number: Vol. 12:0-404-10112-7
International Standard Series Number: 0270-1448

All AMS Books are printed on acid-free paper that meets the guidelines for performance and durability of the Committee on Production Guidelines for Book Longevity of the Council on Library Resources.

Manufactured in the United States of America

AMS Press, Inc.
56 East 13th Street
New York, N.Y. 10003

CONTENTS

INTRODUCTION

CIVIL RIGHTS IN SCHOOLS

Civil rights in education were defined and developed through litigation, an adversarial approach that led to judicial opinions defining constitutional rights and eventually to statutory mandates for fair treatment in schools free of bias based on race, gender, disability, or other classifications. While this approach was necessary to establish rights, another approach to providing people in schools with fairness and education is emerging. Recent research and practice relating to restructuring—or changing the way schools are organized—and to changing the culture or social organization suggest that cooperation and community building are the most effective ways to teach and to learn. The goal of this book is to rethink civil rights in light of current research and policy. The articles trace the legal history of civil rights, analyze its effects on the schools, and suggest alternatives to the adversarial nature of lawsuits.

Ever since President Lyndon Johnson's Great Society programs, the federal government has been involved in all aspects of education. The Elementary and Secondary Education Act of 1965, still on the books, set out the basis of national policy: schools were places where social goals would be met. Congress would pass laws that were supposed to provide equal opportunity for students who had traditionally been excluded from good schools to obtain an education. Through its major provision, now known as "Chapter 1," programs would be devised and funded to help so-called disadvantaged children. Similar laws, such as the Education for All Handicapped Children Act of 1975, tried to provide benefits to disabled students. Title IX and Title VI were passed to prevent discrimination related to sex and race, respectively. Other programs were mandated to help children who do not speak English.

These entitlements, and their underlying philosophy, remained unchallenged until the 1980s. President Ronald Reagan rejected the previous goals, known in education policy circles as "equity," and began to promote his ideas, called "excellence." Instead of developing social programs to provide access to equal educational opportunity, the Reagan and Bush administrations emphasized standards for children already going to school. The government endorsed goals for student achievement, to be evaluated by standardized testing, a national curriculum, merit pay for teachers whose students score high on tests, and continuous retesting to determine if teachers know the material they are supposed to teach. Schools were treated as businesses; the bottom line would be shown by test scores.

Through his campaign statements and political organization, the Democratic Leadership Council (DLC), President Clinton has indicated that he will follow another route to change schools. The New Covenant he proposed in his nomination acceptance speech, as well as the DLC's book *Mandate for Change,* suggests that he will ground his policies in his belief that schools are communities where all who work in or are affected by them must take responsibility for creating the education they seek. He has proposed three major initiatives.

Charter schools and public school choice. Charter schools are places where parents, students, and administrators can set up experimental programs that meet their local needs. While national performance standards should be set up, local districts would be free to use federal funds in a flexible way. Unlike George Bush, who proposed that public funds be spent on private and public school choice, Clinton would limit the use of funds to public school choice. The idea here is that leaving choice to the marketplace will cause wealthier white parents to take some federal money and apply it to private schools, leaving underfunded public schools to minorities and the poor.

Institute Youth Apprenticeship Programs. Half of America's young people do not attend college and are, for the most part, left without the appropriate skills to get a job in an economy that has drastically changed since the old-fashioned vocational programs of the past. For these students, the DLC has proposed a program of classroom instruction to be combined with on-the-job training at a business. Upon completion of the program, students would be certified in their field of expertise. Preparing students for the knowledge-based service and high-tech manufacturing industries, which are the basis of the world economy, would reverse the poor job prospects that now exist, even for those who graduate only from high school.

Enact a civilian "G.I. Bill" for education. This program is related to President Clinton's goals for national service for young people. A youth "Citizens Corps" would be created to involve students in work on the nation's most serious problems. In return, volunteers would earn vouchers for college or job training. If the program works, it should also instill responsibility and a sense of community in participants.

President Clinton's education ideas are a combination of the social program approach with that of the business model tried by the Reagan and Bush administrations. These ideas are not new. But what is intriguing is the special emphasis on creating an ongoing sense of responsibility—a special relationship with the student's community—rather than on merely providing services to individual students. If schools are really allowed to change at the local level to meet the needs of the community and if students know that they can help society and be rewarded, a new view of citizenship can be developed through the education system.

To bring about such reform, the community at large needs to promote and enforce civil rights. If all members of the education community are treated wih dignity and disputes are resolved in an atmosphere of trust and individual responsibility, a foundation will be established for the cooperation that is necessary for education to work. The purpose of this collection is to describe the major issues in civil rights that have arisen in education law and how they have and will affect education practice.

Patricia First provides an overview of civil rights laws in education and describes how school reform must include a strong sense of community. Robert Dentler describes how desegregation has reformed educational policy in the United States and, with Boston as a framework, resulted in more power sharing among community members. Ronald Corwin and Dentler then address one of the most hotly debated issues in education—the use of vouchers that permit parents to use public money to send their children to private schools. In their view, vouchers will undermine public education by harming common societal values. Tedi Mitchell discusses students' due process rights, providing empirical data measuring the effects of court decisions that required fair treatment of students when discipline is administered. She concludes that most school administrators believe the community is best served when students are treated fairly. Jacqueline Stefkovich describes efforts to keep the school community safe through fair search-and-seizure guidelines and suggests alternative models to accomplish this goal. Katherine Hanson's research reports that Title IX of the Education Amendments of 1972 has changed schools for the better for men and women by stressing nondiscrimination based on gender. Kathleen Lynch and Steve Goldberg describe the effects that the Individuals with Disabilities Education Act, formerly the Education for All Handicapped Children Act of 1975, has had on the structure and culture of schools. Finally, Goldberg describes alternate dispute resolution techniques in an essay that proposes that the adversarial approach was necessary to create civil rights, but that negotiation or mediation may be useful for creating a community where fair treatment is likely to occur.

These chapters provide a provocative beginning for rethinking students' rights. If new research on policy implementation, restructuring, and law is taken in account, civil rights will be strengthened because schools will be communities of respect and cooperation.

RONALD G. CORWIN is Professor Emeritus, The Ohio State University, and Director of the METRO Center, Southwest Regional Laboratory. He received his Ph.D. from the University in 1960, and joined the faculty of The Ohio State University, from which he retired in March 1994 as Professor of Sociology. Dr. Corwin is the author of seven books, several research monographs, and numerous scholarly papers and articles in the field of sociology. Dr. Corwin has received national recognition as an outstanding scholar in the fields of sociology of education and education administration. He has served as associated edtor of *Sociology of Education.*

ROBERT DENTLER is Emeritus Professor of Sociology at the University of Massachusetts and is a nationally known authority on school desegregation.

PATRICIA FIRST is Professor and Chair of the Department of Educational Leadership at Western Michigan University. She is a prolific author of articles relating to education law topics and is the founding editor of the *Journal For a Just and Caring Education.* She is on the authors' committee of *West's Education Law Reporter* and is a member of the Board of Directors of the National Organization on Legal Problems in Education.

STEVEN S. GOLDBERG is Professor and Coordinator of the Graduate Educational Leadership Program at Beaver College in Philadelphia and a Lecturer in Education Law at the University of Pennsylvania and Rutgers Law School at Camden, NJ. He is interested in the consequences of imposing law on educational institutions and the uses of mediation to resolve school based disputes. An attorney in the field of education law, he received his Ph.D. from the University of Pennsylvania and a law degree from Brooklyn Law School.

KATHERINE HANSON is associate director of the Center for Equity and Cultural Diversity at Education Development Center, Inc. She directs the Women's Educational Equity Act Publishing Center. Ms. Hanson has conducted research on gender socialization and its implications for institutions. She has authored numerous articles and publications on the subject of gender equity, and has served on the National Coalition for Sex Equity in Education in a leadership capacity. She is currently editing a book on gender equity and middle schools.

KATHLEEN KELLEY LYNCH holds a Ph.D. in Educational Leadership from the University of Pennsylvania, and a Certificate of Advanced Graduate Study in Special Education Administration from Boston University. She is currently Assistant Superintendent of Schools in Exeter, NH. Prior to her tenure in Exeter, she was a Senior Researcher at Education Development Center, Inc. and served as a Director of Pupil Personnel Services, principal, and teacher in public and private schools in several states. She currently teaches in the Graduate School at Rivier College and has taught at the University of New Hampshire, Chestnut Hill College, and Notre Dame College. She has published articles and authored papers on special education, school reform, and education law issues.

TEDI K. MITCHELL, a former secondary school teacher, received her Ph.D. from the University of California, specializing in educational policy, politics, and law. She has taught at U.C.L.A. and lectures on school law at the University of California, Riverside. She is co-author of *Work Orientation and Job Performance.*

JACQUELINE STEFKOVICH is Associate Profesor of Educational Leadership and Policy at Temple University, where she specializes in Fourth Amendment issues in the schools. She received her doctorate in Administration, Planning and Social Policy from Harvard University and a law degree from the University of Pennsylvania.

STUDENT RIGHTS:
FROM CLICHÉ TO SPIRIT

Patricia F. First

For a quarter century the phrase "student rights" has meant the rights of children (and sometimes their parents) to privileges that in the larger meaning of life are rather trivial. I am referring to questions of such issues as hair length, variation in dress, and the use of speech objectionable or vulgar to some people. There are student rights civil libertarians for whom I have great respect who will take issue with such a stand, and I understand and am even sympathetic to their stance that civil liberties must be protected for children as well as adults. Yet in the twenty-five years that discussion of the term "student rights" has meant rights on such a level, more important rights—much more important rights I would argue—have languished.

THE PROBLEM

Twenty-five years of argument over children's expression in its various forms has created a smokescreen of care and concern for children and their rights. In this same time frame the statistics on how Americans treat their children make a lie of this professed concern for students' rights. This mock concern begins with our federal policies. Consider the budget items

1

from the federal government's 1992 budget: Each hour during that fiscal year $33.7 million was spent on national defense, $23.6 million on the national debt, $8.7 million on the savings and loan bailout, $2.9 million on education, and $1.8 million on children's health. Such numbers are morally shocking. They also indicate poor management. Research now shows that every dollar invested in preventive health care for mothers and children saves more than $3 later. Every dollar put into quality preschool education like Head Start saves $4.75 later (Edelman, 1992).

The smokescreen of concern for our children extends to our state and local government and into the home itself. At the state level, more than three decades of attempts to reform school funding formulas have bogged down in battles of will between state courts and state legislatures. The provision of an adequate education for every child is still wishful thinking. Even when the courts have referred to educational adequacy, they have done so in the sense of minimum adequacy (First and Miron, 1991).

At the local level school boards allow the "at risk" phenomenon to grow. One million students drop out of school each year. Fifteen percent of graduates of urban high schools read at less than the sixth-grade level. And in the saddest of statistics, children are not safe even in their own homes. More than two million cases of child abuse and neglect are reported each year: "While the proportion of children in our society declines, the number of children who are living in poverty, homelessness, and situations of abuse and neglect is increasing steadily" (Davis and McCaul, 1991, p. 5).

STEPS TOWARD CHANGE

To correct these ills, educational institutions and the other agencies that affect children and their families must fundamentally change how they organize and function. Such fundamental change requires the reexamination of the ethical structure under which the institutions, and the individuals within them, have been operating. What is required is a new concept of student rights and a recapturing of the spirit of student rights, which entails approaching rights as what we (the society, the country, the schools, the parents, and all of us as individuals) owe our students, rather than what they are allowed to do. This goal can begin with the provision of justice and care for every child.

JUSTICE AND CARE

According to Rawls (1971), justice is the set of principles that all rational human beings would select to govern social behavior if they knew that the rules could potentially apply to themselves. Justice for each student is a cornerstone of the spirit of student rights. And so also is the concept of care.

Since 1971 important work has been done that distinguishes between a "justice orientation focused on identifying and prioritizing conflicting rights or claims" (Gilligan, Ward and Taylor, 1988, xxi) and a "care orientation focused on identifying needs and creating a solution responsive to the needs of all involved" (Gilligan, 1982). This "care orientation" truly encompasses the concept of what I believe educators need to do in order to bring the spirit of student rights to all children. Bringing these rights to children is an ethical imperative for educators (First, 1993). The concept of student rights needs to include the additional emphasis on "care, concern and connectedness" (Martin, 1992), which each child deserves in the care orientation to morality described by Gilligan. Simply put, justice entitles each child to care, concern, and connection in a supportive environment. Each child is entitled to an adequate (not minimally adequate) education in the presence of this care, concern, and connection. These are the important student rights, the ones worth arguing about, striving toward, and fighting over.

At times, an individual educator's moral decisions conflict with what our society has deemed acceptable ethics for our profession. For example, racial discrimination of some children is not legally (rights denied), ethically (justice denied), or morally (care and concern denied) defensible in a school no matter what personal beliefs the teacher or principal may hold. Yet, even in 1992, the system tolerates both subtle and blatant examples of such prejudice within the school rooms and halls. Such discrimination raises the question of institutional ethics and the moral responsibility of the guardians of our educational institutions, the local board members, to bring justice in the form of the crucial student rights to all our children (First and Walberg, 1992).

In the remainder of this chapter, I will provide examples of where justice and care have been denied to girls, the homeless, and minorities. These examples will be followed by a discussion of some of the pressures that have allowed the denial of important student rights to occur in our educational system, actions that need to be taken to bring justice and care to all our children, and the task of ethical educational leaders.

JUSTICE DENIED AND THE ABSENCE OF CARE

Girls: Are They Safe in Our Schools?

The past twenty years have brought many legal victories for girls in our schools, but sometimes the very victories have brought us shocking examples of how unsafe, both physically and psychologically, many schools are for our nation's girls. In an unsafe setting, the student is not experiencing her rights. Two recent court cases provide examples of the safety issue; a description of the newest work on adolescent psychological development will explain the issue of psychological safety. Injustices in the physical and psychological realms are blatant examples of how justice, care, and student rights are denied to girls in our schools.

On a more subtle level, gender discrimination can be seen in an ordinary visit to a generally recognized "good" school. In visiting a pretty, pleasant, suburban school last spring I was shocked to see kindergarten boys always acting as the line leaders and only girls serving in the kindergarten clean-up squads. In the first grade girls only were asked to put aside their own work to help only boys, surely a perversion of peer tutoring. In 1983 Best described a similar scene in a first-grade classroom. A decade seems not to have made much difference in the chances girls have of receiving their legal and ethical right to achieve their own potential and in the chances both boys and girls have of receiving their ethical right to learn helping behavior toward all, regardless of gender.

In the spring of 1992, Title IX, the major protection for girls in their fight for equality in schooling, received a twentieth-anniversary present. On February 26, 1992, the Supreme Court strengthened the protections of Title IX of the Education Amendments of 1972 in deciding that the implied right of action for sexual discrimination under Title IX supports a claim for monetary damages. Though Title IX has prohibited sex discrimination in schools receiving federal funds for twenty years, the lack of a real remedy— a money remedy—has kept it from being a major deterrent to sex discrimination. This unanimous ruling was important because it provides the victims of sex discrimination with this needed meaningful remedy that will spur school boards and administrators to guard against such misconduct (First and Rossow, 1992a).

The case of *Franklin v. Gwinnett County Public Schools* (112 S. Ct. 1028) is a warning to school boards and administrators of the dangers of ignoring or treating lightly students' rights in the form of complaints of sexual harassment by teachers. Christine Franklin was subjected to continual sexual harassment beginning in the tenth grade from Andrew Hill, a sports coach and teacher in the Gwinnett County Public Schools. Incidents ranged from sexually oriented conversations to Hill's interrupting a class, requesting that the teacher excuse Franklin, and taking her to a private office where he subjected her to coercive intercourse. Perhaps most shocking to concerned parents and educators is the information that school officials became aware of and investigated this harassment but took no action to stop it. Franklin was even discouraged from pressing charges against Hill.

Franklin won her case, but no doubt the harm of being raped at school will be a lifelong tragedy. Her case is not isolated. It is spectacular only in that it reached the Supreme Court. This decision came just as the sexual harassment of schoolgirls was receiving increased attention. A *New York Times* article, "The Schools, the Newest Arena for Sex-Harassment Concerns" 11 March 1992, called attention to a report released by the American Association of University Women that year that painted a damning picture of how girls are treated in schools. The report found an increase in sexual harassment in schools as early as the seventh grade. AAUW Executive Director Anne Bryant said that schools have an obligation to protect girls from harassment by teachers or other students: "No girl should have to deal with sexual harassment in the classroom, corridors or playground of her school." Bryant noted that one of the recommendations for action in the AAUW report is the development of strong policies against sexual harassment to be enforced by school personnel and supported by "the Supreme Court ruling [that] now gives school districts across America a financial, as well as moral, imperative to do so immediately."

The treatment of girls in disciplinary cases also raises ethical questions. To include care and concern as a standard of just treatment may allow the courts eventually to find legal what the educator may still find unethical. If we accept Rawl's (1971) definition of justice as the set of principles that all rational human beings would select to govern social behavior if they knew that the rules could potentially apply to themselves, would any of us want our daughter to undergo the following ordeal?

For the first time in history, a court upheld the strip search of a student. A unanimous United States Court of Appeals for the Sixth Circuit affirmed a summary judgment of the United States District Court for the Western District of Kentucky. The case, *Williams by Williams v. Ellington,* (936 F. 2nd 881, 6th Cir. 1991), marks the eleventh time a student strip search has been litigated. Since the first case was decided in 1973, no court until *Williams* has been willing to uphold this highly intrusive search method (First and Rossow, 1992b).

In *Williams,* a female Kentucky high school student was suspected of being in possession of "rush." While the substance can be purchased over the counter, it is defined as a volatile substance, and its inhalation is illegal under the state law. After a week-long investigation by school authorities, Williams's locker was searched along with several other girls' suspected of being in possession of rush. No drugs were found. At that time the principal, Jerald Ellington, ordered Assistant Principal Maxine Easley to conduct a personal search of Williams in the presence of a female secretary. Inside Easley's office, Williams was asked to empty her pockets, which she promptly did. Easley then asked the girl to remove her T-shirt.

Although she hesitated and appeared nervous, Williams complied after Easley repeated the request. Williams was then required to lower her blue jeans to her knees. In her deposition, Williams testified that Easley pulled on the elastic of her undergarments to see if anything would fall out, but Easley disputes this contention. Finally, Williams was told to remove her shoes and socks. No evidence of drugs was found.

In both the *Franklin* and *Williams* cases the very institution that could be a haven, a place exhibiting Martin's 3 C's of care, concern, and connectedness, is the place a girl finds sexual abuse and lack of concern. The educators in these cases violated both commonly accepted personal morality and the ethics of their profession. These girls were denied the spirit of student rights. It is terribly sad that these are not isolated cases, but even more widespread is the neglect of the newest research about girls' development.

The resistance to study and incorporate the newest work on the psychological development of girls is unexplainable except as a perversion of the educator's ethical responsibility to be up-to-date both in content and pedagogy for the good of all our children. Gilligan's work enlarges the field of developmental psychology to include the experiences of diverse racial and ethnic groups as well as the experiences of girls (Gilligan, 1982; 1988). Gilligan says we continue to study adolescent boys and make generalizations about human development, but when girls are studied researchers get a very different view. She insists that traditional judgments about the nature of human development be suspended until further research is done. This is just one example of work by a significant theorist and researcher that is virtually ignored in schooling. "She has been one of the most visible and convincing proponents of an alternative perspective to the traditional ideas of psychology, ideas expounded by men about men yet claiming to represent the entire human condition" (Csikszentmihalyi, 1989).

The traditional and now very outdated way girls are regarded in far too many schools is ethically unconscionable and is a distinct denial of their rights. Educators should know by now that "girls' abiding concern for human relatedness and personal responsibility is not a lower form of reasoning, but an equally sophisticated and vital perspective, complementing the more masculine concerns for rights and justice" (Csikszentmihalyi, 1989). Yet in classrooms everyday, girls' moral development is devalued as they are cajoled and corrected to be more objective, less personal, in other words, to be like the boys. On a crowded planet beset by seemingly unsolvable social issues, one must ponder why an ideal of hardness, independence, detachment, autonomy, and distancing from both other people's and one's own emotions is still seen as desirable for either boys or girls. In making schools more ethical places that exhibit care, concern, connectedness, and respect for student rights, we must emancipate our thinking from the biases of institutional self-interest. In so doing, let us make the school a warmer, less complicated, and more harmonious place.

Homeless: Is the Schoolhouse Open?

The plight of the homeless is recognized as a national emergency. The news media continually bring the crisis to our attention. The numbers are staggering. Jonathan Kozol (1988) has estimated that between two and three million people are without homes in the United States. It is more conservatively estimated that at least 100,000 children are homeless on any given night, among a total of approximately 750,000 homeless people (National Academy of Sciences, 1988). In 1987, the National Coalition of the Homeless reported that families with children were the fastest growing segment of the homeless population, and that 40 percent of the homeless population consists of families. About 500,000 children are homeless. Of these homeless children, 4370 do not attend school, primarily because of residency requirements (National Coalition of the Homeless, 1987). The focus here is the plight of the homeless children specifically as it relates to access to schooling. That these children have been, and are, denied access to schooling because of their homeless state is well documented (First and Cooper, 1989). The main reasons for such denial—residency requirements, transportation needs, lost records, the timelines for special education placement, and substantiated guardianship—are generally well within the legal operating parameters of the school districts involved. But the case of homeless children is a particularly poignant example of the difficult choices facing education agencies when legally defensible positions do not coincide with what many would believe to be morally responsible positions. For a homeless child, the school is a hope and a refuge, for the present as well as the future.

In July 1987 significant legislation to address needs of the homeless was signed into law in the form of the Stewart B. McKinney Homeless Assistance Act. This law provided comprehensive federal emergency assistance for homeless persons and specifically addressed the barriers to education of homeless children. Hopes were high that the McKinney Act would quickly lower the barriers erected between homeless children and their only real hope for the future, access to school, but most of the nation's schools have not responded with care, concern, and connectedness for the nation's neediest children.

The states responded with state plans to access the McKinney funds, and they continue to file those plans. The barriers facing homeless children as they attempt to go to school have already forced some rethinking of the fundamental goals, the priorities, and the funding of public schooling.

However, the state plans, even the best of them, do not fulfill a reformer's dream of the public school's becoming an advocate for children, particularly poor and homeless children. Instead, these plans illustrate responsive instrumentalists. The responses vary from excellent to poor or even nonexistent. Even in excellent plans, there is not an advocacy and coordinating role for children, and the school may be the only agency positioned to fill that particular societal need (First and Cooper, 1990).

It is hard to say if the McKinney Act has helped the homeless. A spokesperson for the National Coalition for the Homeless in Washington said that it has to some extent stirred action, but that the Act has not been stringently enforced and the enforcement has not addressed quality of content (Alker, 1989). Conversations with the U.S. Department of Education homeless coordinator confirmed that enforcement of the McKinney Act has been limited to minimum compliance, and even state participation to that level has been deemed voluntary (Fagan, 1989). The reality today is that the large numbers of homeless children are growing up uneducated. Little children are homeless on our streets, their life chances drastically curtailed (First, 1992). We see in the case of homeless children ethical gaps in the institutional responses of all levels of educational governance, as well as questionable ethics at the more individual levels within a given school district.

Having homeless children in the classroom confronts one daily with the painful consideration of ethical and moral questions. We still have school board members, superintendents, principals, and teachers who have not heard of the McKinney Act, or who think it does not affect their schools, or who cannot believe that these people really have no place to go at night. One said to me recently about a supply fee, "But it's only $2 per child." As the old saying goes, many of us would benefit from a walk in the other's shoes. Can such people be serious about protecting student rights, or are they likely simply to allow diversity in dress and believe they have attended to student rights? Denying homeless children access to that classroom is to make a terrible ethical choice.

Minorities: Must We Have Racism in the Schoolhouse?

If the progress of girls' rights in our schools over the twenty years since Title IX is discouraging, then surely the progress of racial minorities in our schools in the thirty-eight years since *Brown v. Board of Education* (1954) is enough to cause despair. In this racist society, to behave ethically as educators we must confront and vanquish our own racism and the entrenched racism of our educational institutions. In the spring of 1992 my attention was riveted, along with the rest of the nation, on the burning of Los

Angeles. Surely our social policy writers, with more space and time than that available to me now, can pose the Watts Riots of 1966 and the burning of Los Angeles in 1992 as brackets between which the national policy to desegregate schools was tried, lauded, and then retracted. Perhaps the social historians will be able to tell us if a different scenario, a whole-hearted commitment to an excellent, integrated education for all our children, could have prevented the maturing of another desperate and violent generation. The people who burned Los Angeles in 1992 were schooled in the educational system of "savage inequalities," so movingly portrayed by Kozol (1991). Will more cities burn before we finally get the message that if all the children do not get a fair chance, their fundamental rights in life, everyone will pay in a terrible way?

That same spring in *Freeman v. Pitts,* a case from DeKalb County, Georgia, the Supreme Court gave hundreds of formerly segregated school districts a potential new legal tool for returning to local control. The ruling allows school districts to win release from court control bit by bit as they achieve racial equality in various facets of their operations. It overturned a federal appeals court ruling that required school districts to achieve equality in seven aspects of their operations before they could win any release from judicial supervision.

Some civil rights advocates saw the decision as a blow to school desegregation efforts, arguing that more conservative judges appointed by Presidents Reagan and Bush would be more likely to let school districts "off the hook," allowing shifts toward resegregation. Others believed the Court made no major departure from previous principles. But all the school desegregation experts interviewed in various new articles said they would have to wait and see how lower courts ruled in the hundreds of school desegregation cases pending across the country.

In many ways, some said, the decision was more notable for what it did not do than what it did. Civil rights advocates had hoped the Court would clear up many of the ambiguities in previous decisions, setting stricter and clearer guidelines for school districts on how long they must continue court-ordered desegregation and how thorough desegregation must be. School districts also wanted clarity but hoped for less stringent rules. Neither side got its wish.

In one of the more interesting interviews in the immediate aftermath of this decision, Kenneth Clark spoke to Nat Hentoff of the *Washington Post* ("Back to Separate but Equal," 11 Apr. 1992). Clark's research, emphasizing that segregation in public schools generates in black children "a feeling of inferiority that may affect their hearts and minds in a way unlikely to ever be undone," was influential in the Court's decision in *Brown v. Board of Education.* Clark said, in reaction to the DeKalb decision, "We

are now not only whittling down *Brown v. Board of Education,* we are moving back to the 'separate but equal doctrine' of *Plessy v. Ferguson.''*
''What the court is saying,'' Clark pointed out, ''is forget *Brown v. Board of Education.* Let's put all that stuff about resegregation aside. What really bothers me is there doesn't seem to be any concern about the children—white or black.''

It is four decades since *Brown* began the era of school desegregation intended to transcend racial divisions. And the result of this widely resented, endlessly litigated effort? Sixty-three percent of black school children attend primarily non-white schools. Thirty-two percent of black students are in schools that are 90 to 100 percent non-white. Sixty-eight percent of Hispanic students—largely ignored by the courts—are in non-white schools. The result is still vast sectors of discrimination in the public schools (First and Rossow, 1992c).

Other groups of students are also still denied justice. For example, justice in the schools has been slow to come to disabled children, and too many must still go to court to force school districts to provide them their rights (Goldberg and Lynch, 1992).

In addition, the number of reported child abuse cases has been increasing in the nation. Abused children, like the homeless, need refuge at school. But the ethics of legally required reporting has not been confronted by schools and educators because this issue has not been conceptualized as a student right. Many school people are reluctant to report, even when directly told by a child that he or she is being abused. And the numbers continue to rise. ''In 1989, approximately 2.4 million child-abuse reports were filed with the National Committee for the Prevention of Child Abuse with more than 400,000 of these reports involving sexual abuse. Also in 1989, state child protection agencies throughout our country reported nearly 1,250 child-abuse related deaths—a 38 percent increase over 1985 (Davis and McCaul, 1991).

These examples, girls, the homeless, minorities, the disabled and abused, are discussed here to shock us into the realization that as of 1992 the educational system is not behaving ethically toward all our children. Justice is too often denied, and our students are not receiving their rights. They are not receiving care.

HOW CAN IT HAPPEN?

Values Left on the Doorstep

Do we leave our values on the doorstep when we go to work? In 1938 Virginia Woolf invited us to stand with her on a bridge and watch the proession of men that moved from private home to public world each morning and back again each night (Martin, 1992). Today, if we focused on school leaders we would watch both men and women leaving their private worlds each morning. But the kinds of questions Woolf asked as she watched the procession are the same kinds of questions we should ask today about the men and women leading our schools. On what terms do they join the public world each morning? As they cross the bridge do they remain "civilized human beings?" Do they bring with them the private world values of care, concern, and connection (Martin, 1992), or do they enter today's "real world," one of possessiveness, jealousy, pugnacity, and greed? The school leader crosses the bridge each morning to lead an institution erected for children, an institution entrusted with children's care and education and growth. Surely there is no institution that needs more to emphasize Martin's 3 C's—care, concern, and connection—and no institution that needs more to be adamant about the protection of student rights.

The Problem of Many Hands

Turning to political ethics we find a possible explanation, though not justification, for the phenomena of values left on the doorstep each morning: the problem of many hands (Thompson, 1987). Thompson writes of hierarchical and collective models as the conventional ways of ascribing responsibility in politics. These are also the ways responsibility is usually ascribed in schools.

In the hierarchical model, responsibility is expected to fall on the person in the highest position in the formal or informal chain of command. But in the real world, acceptance of responsibility is mitigated by the fact that implementation and further decision making is passed through many levels up and down the chain of command. Under the collective-responsibility model, outcomes are the product of the actions of many different people. Individual contributions may be difficult to distinguish at all and cannot easily be separated from the contributions of many other people.

These two models taken together help to explain why educational malpractice has not yet been provable in court. By the time a child is so far behind in skills that a parent takes action, the child has had many different teachers (collective-responsibility model), and those teachers have been subject to the rulings of many different administrators (hierarchical model and collective-responsibility model). The two models taken together also help us to understand how educators, who may as individuals decry the kind of ethical problems we have discussed, allow such situations to continue in their own schools and classrooms. They do indeed leave their values on the doorstep each morning. They feel powerless to do anything about such immense problems because of the hierarchical establishment they face and the tradition of collective responsibility in our profession.

And yet, in a profession the professional takes responsibility for his or her actions, in this instance the outcomes in the lives of all children. Thompson argues that these conventional ways of ascribing responsibility, the hierarchical and collective-responsibility models, "are not satisfactory responses to the problem of many hands; and that personal responsibility, properly interpreted, can be imputed to officials more often than these models imply" (1987, 40). Our profession must face squarely the problems of many hands and assign individual educators the expectation and responsibility of "doing the right thing" (Lee, 1989).

Spike Lee's characters in his 1989 film *Do the Right Thing* struggled with ethical and moral decisions around how to treat each other in their neighborhood. Roger Ebert's description of this struggle in Lee's film could apply to the daily struggle of educators in the school place: "Of course it is confused. Of course it wavers between middle-class values and street values. Of course it is not sure whether it believes in liberal pieties, or militancy. Of course some of the characters are sympathetic and others are hateful—and of course some of the likable characters do bad things. Isn't that the way it is in America today?" (1992, 62). But sympathetic or hateful, all children deserve their rights.

Common Pressures

If one does not keep stressing respect for meaningful student rights, educational leaders can slide into a sort of reverse (or preverse) pride in protecting the institution instead of the children. For example, they may celebrate "winning" a challenge from a parent of a special education student, thus saving the district money, without considering whether or not they have really served the child, whether or not they have denied that child's rights. Much is justified in the name of saving the district money such as turning away a homeles child in direct violation of the McKinney Homeless Assistance Act because that child's parents cannot prove residence in the district. In such a case, money saved for the district is a right denied to the neediest of the needy and the most helpless to complain.

In the course of decision-making, the administrator must remember that the goal is justice, care, concern, and connectedness for all children. Strike, Haler, and Soltis (1985) provide a scenario where an administrator is confronted with an ethical dilemma regarding parental pressure. According to the scenario, it is common knowledge in the district that one teacher at a particular grade level is better than the other. Each year the parents of the wealthier children are the ones who want to be sure that their children get the better teacher. But at other grade levels placement decisions are made on a range of factors. If the principal acquiesces to the parental pressure, the better teacher at this grade level will have better prepared students with more helpful parents. The children who need that good teacher the most will be grouped together with the less able teacher. It is district ethos to please the parents when possible, but justice for all children demands not pleasing the parents in this case. What to do?

Does it really matter, matter in a big way, matter enough to justify possible "trouble" from superintendent or board or both? In those children's lives will one better teacher in one grade make a significant difference? Well, maybe, maybe not. But it is argued here that justice and care for all children demands that all children always be given their chance. We cannot gaze into the future and know which one of our decisions really matters. But as many things in this world add up to the good, or to success incrementally, so does the development of a meaningful conception of student rights for all children. A decision made in this case in favor of the less fortunate children, added to countless other decisions made in the name of student rights for all children, may make enormous differences in one or many lives. As school leaders, our duty is to make the ethical decision and cast that bit of good into the world's milieu.

WHAT WE MUST DO

Respect Families

We must do for all our children what their parents do not. In most of our public schools we do more of what the parents are already doing for the fortunate children. Those who need us the most are the most neglected. The idea of doing more for the neediest is hardly new. In 1781, Johann Pestalozzi wrote, "You should do for your children what their parents failed to do for them."

Perhaps it would help us to start with a change in attitude toward parents who are not doing all we think they should for their children. A climate of acceptance rather than condemnation would be a starting place for the ethical treatment of all children.

To provide children with justice and care, educators must provide them, and their families, with respect. An area educators could work on quickly is to expand their concept of family and indicate respect for the variety of family forms the children before them might be coming from each morning. Educators tend to come from conservative backgrounds, but no matter how individually difficult it is for them, they must learn to accept a broader array of family types if they are to provide justice for all children. A student has the right to expect respect for herself and her family.

According to the Bureau of Census (1991) only 25.9 percent of U.S. households in 1991 consist of the traditional married couple with their own child or children under age 18. Half of all marriages end in divorce. Births to single mothers now make up one-quarter of total births. One in four Americans over age 18 have never married. These factors have whittled away at the number of households that fit the traditional model.

In bringing justice to all children, respect for their families must be extended to include blended families, extended families, various arrangements of guardianship, chosen families, and all other supportive kinship systems. There are legions of parents who feel unwelcome at school, yet both research literature and popular wisdom make us aware that home and school must be partners for all our children. It is the educated educators who bear the moral and ethical responsibility to break down these barriers, to suspend judgmental words and body language, and to leave at home all personal, moral, and religious convictions about their students family arrangements. Such acceptance is an important component of the new concept of student rights.

Provide Small Victories

Part of the ethical deliberations of any school-site faculty should revolve around the whole area of standards, success, and how to provide "small victories" for every child (Freedman, 1990). We can no longer take for granted the "rightness" of standards and ways of measurement that have been handed down from the hierarchical past. "Our literature is full of studies of gender and race that examine the deficiencies of minorities and women in meeting the standards of success as defined by a society that has historically excluded minorities and women in the construction of the standards by which they are measured" (Brickhouse, 1989, 14).

The movement toward alternative assessment is a positive one in light of ethical considerations for both the individual educator and the profession. It need not be discouraged by the seemingly countertrend toward national assessment and international comparison. It is our ethical responsibility as a profession to define ethically supportable standards at all levels for all our children.

What is not being suggested here is reliance upon a rigid, legalistic, and ethical code in order to provide respect for student rights. Just as Punch (1986) suggests that ethical codes fail to solve the situational ethics of field research and threaten to restrict considerably a great deal of research, so too in the very personal and individualistic atmosphere of school and classroom would rigidity of code be troublesome. Delivering rights to all children will take the educational leader into a potentially vast range of social

social settings and experiences with unpredictable problems and consequences. In each school setting, leaders can take the initiative in developing consensus on the specific ethical considerations that setting provides and on the specific problems that school's constituency brings to the school. The political, the personal, and the ethical factors will vary in each setting, though there will be close resemblance in agreed-upon professional ethics across the educational field. Ultimately, each educator must become his or her own moral decision maker within the expanded and accepted ethics of the profession. Remembering Martin's third C, connectedness, will help a faculty work on the relation building needed to facilitate the dialogue on student rights.

Prepare for Ethical Reasoning

Now is the time for programs of preparation for both teachers and administrators to face squarely the need for training in ethical decision making and its relationship to a new conceptualization of student rights. The best and most vital programs today are doing so. Good preparation programs can help people learn moral reasoning and to recognize when consciously to apply it. Good preparation programs can help people recognize the ethical dilemmas of their society and consider how schools and educators can contribute to the solutions.

"Thus it is crucial that people be able to reflect ethically on their choices and their actions. This is especially important when individuals have power and influence over the lives of others. We can think of few areas where it is more important than in the administration of schools." (Strike, Haller, and Soltis, 1988, 6).

Making the School Ethical

The ethical climate of the school helps to determine which issues organization members consider to be ethically pertinent, and what criteria they use to understand, weigh, and resolve these issues. All organizational values that pertain to questions of right and wrong contribute to the ethical climate of the company: the shared perceptions of what is correct behavior (i.e., content), and how ethical issues will be dealt with (i.e., process) (Cullen, Victor, and Stephens, 1989). A climate that is low on caring could create an environment in which children are treated in callous and potentially illegal ways. Such a climate will lower motivation for both educators and students and will not offer a haven of respected student rights.

So what can the school leader do to change the organizational climate? If that leader is currently in an influential management position, much can potentially be done. "Management can strengthen and change the ethical climate through education and training in ethical decision making; revision or development of a formal corporate code of ethics; changes in monitoring and supervision; and alternations in company policies, procedures, manuals, performance objectives, selection processes, and incentive structures." (Cullen, Victor, and Stephens, 1989, 61).

Faculty members can also do much to change the climate of the organization. Faculty members, by talking with and listening to each other, can better understand themselves and their responsibilities in the world of the school. Educators can gain moral strength "to do the right thing" (Lee, 1989) by becoming a part of a web of relationships at the school site. Persons in supportive and caring environments, taking time to listen to and learn from each other, are more likely to explore and consider carefully the difficult moral choices faced each day by an educator, as well as the ethical questions confronting our profession as a whole. In the web of organizational ties there will be sympathetic people to help when the problems confront us (Helgesen, 1990).

Some current reforms may be pointing us in the right direction. At its best the movement toward school-site managment is an opportunity to refocus the school to an ethics of care, concern, and connectedness, to the goal of delivering rights to every child. A cosmetic shift to school-site management is merely a shift of some power in an otherwise undisturbed hierarchy. Noddings words may help us understand the relational ethic to be found in an organizational web of care and concern. "A relational ethic remains tightly tied to experience because all its deliberations focus on the human beings involved in the situation under consideration and their relations to each other" (Noddings, 1988, 218).

CONCLUSION

The timing is right to do what must be done to make our schools respect student rights. Society as a whole and its organizations are in the middle of a shift from the bureaucratic to the democratic ethos—part of the paradigm shift that has been described by both scholars and popular writers. Thus the difficulty of today's ethical questions is not an issue unique to our field (Hejka-Ekins, 1988).

Under the bureaucratic ethos organizations operated under five classic Weberian ethical standards: efficiency, competence, loyalty, expertise, and accountability. Most professional codes of ethics were built upon these five standards. Operating under this ethos, organizations could more easily "avoid" the ethical issues because objectivity became a defense. The ideal of administration was considered value neutrality, and a school administrator was considered a functionary removed from value judgments. The teacher of course was expected to do what she was told, and in too many school districts these dated stereotypes are still operationalized.

The democratic ethos is being built upon four ethical standards: constitutional values such as free speech, due process, and equal protection of law; public interest; citizenship; and social equality. Being in the middle of such a fundamental shift means lack of, or difficulty obtaining, consensus on everyday operating norms and the confusion of operating under a double standard in everyday life. Respect for the rights of our students to justice, care, connectedness, and concern must be a school priority in this time of transition.

It is time to rethink the phrase "student rights" or to find a new term for a new century. It is time to focus the energies of the educational community and society as a whole on what we owe students, "we" being the society at large exercising its response to student rights through the structure of educational institutions. What do we owe them—these students who come shyly but eagerly to kindergarten and exit secondary school too often crushed in spirit and opportunity?

We owe them kindness and care, respect for themselves, their heritage, and their families. We owe them sanctuary if they are among the over two million children abused and neglected in their homes, and we owe them safety while they are in our care. We owe them shelter if they are among the more than 100,000 homeless children on any given night. We owe them cleanliness and functioning buildings, equipment for the best education for every child, and beauty. Yes, we owe them beauty in their days, a setting where one's best can flourish. We owe them an adequate education. Every school board in every city and town owes the best of today's and tomorrow's education to every child in its care. The spirit of student rights demands it.

REFERENCES

Alker, J. 1989. Interview with author. 25 Oct.

American Association of University Women. 1992. *How schools shortchange girls: A study of major findings in girls and education.* Washington, D.C.: AAUW Education Foundation.

Beck, C. 1990. *Better schools: A values perspective.* Philadelphia: Falmer Press.

Best, R. 1983. *We've all got scars.* Bloomington: Indiana University Press.

Brickhouse, N. 1989. Ethics in field-based research: Contractual and relational responsibilities. Annual meeting of the National Association for Research in Science Teaching.

Bureau of the Census. 1991. *Household and Family Characteristics: March 1991*. Washington, D.C.: U.S. Department of Commerce.

Csikszentmihalyi, M. 1989. More ways than one to be good. *The New York Times Book Review*, 28 May, 6.

Cullen, J., B. Victor, and C. Stephens. 1989. An ethical weather report: Assessing the organization's ethical climate. *Organizational Dynamics* 50–62.

Davis, W., and E. McCaul. 1991. *The emerging crisis: Current and projected status of children in the United States*. Orono, ME: Institute for the Study of At-Risk Children, University of Maine.

Ebert, R. 1992. *Roger Ebert's movie home companion*. Kansas City: Andrews & McMeel.

Edelman, M. W. 1992. *The measure of our success: A letter to my children and yours*. Boston: Beacon Press.

Fagan, T. 1989. Interview with author. 25 Oct.

First, P. 1993. Ethics in school administration: Leaders who know right from wrong. *People and Education*, 1 (2), 126–50.

First, P. 1992. The reality: The status of education for homeless children and youth. In *Educating America's homeless children and youth: Policy and practice*, ed. J. Stronge. Beverly Hills, CA: Sage.

First, P., and G. Cooper. 1989. Access to education by homeless children. *Education Law Reporter* 53:757–65.

———. 1990. The McKinney Homeless Assistance Act: Evaluating the response of the states. *Education Law Reporter* 60:1047–60.

First, P., and L. Miron. 1991. The social construction of adequacy. *Journal of Law and Education* 20:421–44.

First, P., and L. Rossow. 1992a. An enormous victory for women and girls. *School Law Reporter* 33:1–2.

———. 1992b. Student strip search upheld. *School Law Reporter* 33:1–2.

———. 1992c. The spring of race riots and the retreat from school desegregation, *School Law Reporter* 33.

First, P., and H. Walberg, eds. 1992. *School boards: Changing local control*. Berkeley, CA: McCutchan.

Fischer, F., and J. Forester, eds. 1987. *Confronting values in policy analysis: The politics of criteria*. Beverly Hills, CA: Sage.

Freedman, S. 1990. *Small victories: The real world of a teacher, her students, & their high school*. New York : Harper & Row.

Gilligan, C. 1982. *In a different voice: Psychological theory and women's development*. Cambridge, MA: Harvard University Press.

Gilligan, C., J. Ward, and J. Taylor, eds. 1988. *Mapping the moral domain*. Cambridge, MA: Harvard University Press.

Goldberg, S., and K. Lynch. 1992. Reconsidering the legalization of school reform: A case for implementing change through mediation. *Ohio State Journal on Dispute Resolution* 7:199–215.

Hejka-Ekins, A. 1988. Teaching ethics in public administration. *Public Administration Review,* 48:885–90.

Helgesen, S. 1990. *The female advantage: Women's ways of leadership.* New York: Doubleday.

Hentoff, N. 1992. Back to separate but equal. *Washington Post,* April 11, 1992.

Keeley, M. 1978. A social justice approach to organizational evaluation. *Administrative Science Quarterly* 23.

Kozol, J. 1988. *Rachel and her children: Homeless families in America.* New York: Crown.

———. 1991. *Savage inequalities: Children in America's schools.* New York: Crown.

Lee, S. 1989. *Do the right thing.* Film produced by Spike Lee.

Martin, J. 1992. *The schoolhome.* Cambridge, MA: Harvard University Press.

National Academy of Sciences. 1988. *Homelessness, health and human needs.* Washington, D.C.: National Academy of Sciences.

National Coalition of the Homeless. 1987. *Broken lives.* Washington, D.C.: National Academy of Sciences.

Noddings, N. 1988. An ethic of caring and its implications for instructional arrangements. *American Journal of Education* 96:215–30.

Pestalozzi, J. 1885. *Leonard and Gertrude.* Boston: D.C. Heath.

Punch, M. 1986. *The politics and ethics of fieldwork.* Beverly Hills, CA: Sage.

The Random House college dictionary New York: Random House, 1980.

Rawls, J. 1971. *A theory of justice.* New York: Belknap Press.

The schools, the newest arena for sex-harassment concerns. *New York Times,* 11 Mar. 1992.

Strike, K., E. Haller, and J. Soltis. 1988. *The ethics of school administration.* New York: Teacher's College Press.

Thompson, D. 1987. *Political ethics and public office.* Cambridge, MA: Harvard University Press.

Woolf, V. 1938. *Three guineas.* New York: Harcourt Brace Jovanovich.

SCHOOL DESEGREGATION IN BOSTON:
A SUCCESSFUL ATTACK ON RACIAL EXCLUSION OR A BUNGLE?

Robert A. Dentler

INTRODUCTION

Although the idea of school desegregation is much older than its contemporary usage, ever since the *Brown v. Board of Education* decision of the U.S. Supreme Court in 1954 it has referred to the actions taken to unify a public school district and the schools and programs within it so that policies and practices or racial duality will be eliminated (Kluger, 1976). The idea can be applied to private schools and to colleges and universities as well, of course. If desegregation plans have been ordered by a court as remedy for the wrongs of racial segregation and discrimination by a state or a locality or institution, those orders in legal principle remain in effect until the court is satisfied that unity has been achieved. Where desegregation takes place because of legislative, executive, or voluntary policy decisions, the standard for completion of the action is similar if less stringent in interpretation.

This chapter traces the historical evolution of racial desegregation of public school districts in the United States. It then focuses on the case of desegregation of the Boston public schools and considers the import of the court-ordered equity reforms in that system over time, giving some extra attention to reform efforts in the realm of special education. It tries to give partial answers to this question: was the Boston public school desegregation case, viewed in the long term, an effective attack on the wrongs of racial exclusion, or was it a case in which reforms were bungled?

HISTORICAL TRENDS

Most lawyers, social scientists, and educators agree (Kirp, 1982) that school desegregation is both a process and an aimed-for condition in which no student is denied access to a campus, school, or program, treated unequally, or isolated or separated in any way on the basis of race or ethnicity. The *Brown* decision originally pertained to remedying the institutional and state-based racial dominance of whites over blacks, but over the years courts and other authorities broadened the policy to include a wide range of other ethnic minorities (Dentler, Mackler and Warschauer, 1967). The initial targets of the federal courts were the public schools of the South and the border states where black students had been excluded from some schools and programs and assigned to others as a matter of state laws dictating racial separation that had been passed in the post-reconstruction era. The *Brown* decision asserted unanimously that these laws were an affront to the rights of black students and a source of permanent harm to their hearts, minds, and educational fates. Most attorneys and educators imagined initially that remedies for this long-standing wrong would consist almost wholly of the redistribution of students, faculty, and staff and a modicum of equalization of facilities and materials and services across school districts. Leading attorneys for the black plaintiffs, including Thurgood Marshall, believed that when white students would be assigned to the historically black schools, their parents would not tolerate the continuation of the extremely substandard conditions and services within them and that their school improvement demands would then lift the quality of educational opportunities for black students (Wolters, 1984).

Over the thirty-five years that followed, school desegregation came to entail many other remedial acts of policy and practice as well. These include finances, curriculum, personnel recruitment and appointment procedures, transportation, discipline codes, safety and security, cocurricular programs, special and bilingual and vocational education, collaboratives with business and colleges and cultural agencies, guidance counseling, school-community relations, and student government, to name a few of the major domains. The expansion of the term race to include a wide range of ethnic minorities and the evolution of court orders and policies to include these many domains, took place because judges and legislators and administrators presiding over the desegregation process came slowly to understand that the layers of racial duality, a legal euphemism for institutional racism, are not only very deep, but also are welded onto the walls and floors of schools and are built into the subculture and personalities of those who inhabit them and run them. As we understand it from the sociology of education, (Persell, 1977), desegregation is a decision and a tool for attacking the roots and branches of structural dominance in teaching and learning systems of all kinds—a dominance that slopes and biases the playing field for learners by the intrusion of race, ethnicity, gender, and social class as somewhat systematically injected handicaps that affect educational attainment, retention, and cognitive achievement. The interventions required are often political rather than technical; they are byproducts of white fears, white defiance, and the avoidance, so that desegregative remedies over time become more or less rigorous and comprehensive as their authors try to prevent or offset prospects of failure, or as they become coopted by dominant groups in the community (Raffel, 1980).

Although social scientists have been significantly involved in work on one or another aspect of desegregation, none has yet produced an authoritative evaluation of its effects. There are a few landmark studies that help in this regard, however. The Coleman survey (Coleman, 1966) identified the comparatively insignificant influence of schooling itself on academic achievement, noting that family background and socioeconomic status accounted for most of the variance in achievement, but also noting that black students were more positively assisted by good schooling than were students from other ethnic groups. Desegregation for Coleman was a matter of demonstrating statistically that black students benefited from the relatively higher quality of predominantly white public schools.

Meyer Weinberg, in 1970 authored a definitive summary and historical interpretation of desegregation progress and student effects, and Nancy St. John, in 1972 did an outstanding meta-review of outcome studies. Willis Hawley (1984) led a massive organized effort to synthesize the knowledge base about school desegregation, while Charles Willie (1984) has demonstrated that good school desegregation plans can accomplish their objectives. We know from these and many other smaller inquiries that school desegregation can lift the average school achievement levels of black students and improve the interpersonal relations between all students when it is well implemented (Miller and Brewer, 1984).

There are gaps, uncertainties, and contradictions in some of the evidence, however. Some desegregation efforts appear from the social scientific record (St. John, 1975) to have no observable benefits, and a few have been found to impede the learning and sometimes even the self-esteem of students (Boardman, 1971). Naive researchers and commentators have often failed to note that school-learning benefits could rarely be expected to accrue from desegregation plans that contained no features designed to generate such benefits. This was generally the case with plans during the 1955 to 1970 phase of actions stemming from the *Brown* decision. In those years a race case, as the federal judges called the school district and state cases under *Brown,* concerned mixing students and staffs and readjusting school facilities and sites and very little else. Other far more complex issues kept evolving and figuring in small ways in individual cases, but it was not until the next phase, from 1971 through 1984, that curricular and instructional remedies became customary. Another factor limiting evaluation research in school desegregation has been the fact that researchers have frequently had to study the intervention within the context of a single school district where the plan may have been poorly conceived, gravely compromised by white resistance, or poorly implemented, or all three, in which event no comparative or analytic examination of effects resulting from a reasoned intervention could be achieved.

These are fairly mild if dismal consequences of flaws in policy, policy execution, or research sensibilities when compared with other disputes that have sprung up over the years, however. The first phase had given segregationists and upholders of the status quo in public education abundant time in which to invent and field-test a virtual lexicon of arguments against school desegregation. Some were updated versions of ideas as old as those used to buttress slavery in the colonies, while others were borrowed from the *Plessy v. Ferguson* era of "separate but equal." Still other arguments, including some developed by social scientists, were fresh outgrowths from the remedies and planning proposals themselves. These are all catalogued reliably in an able if ideologically rabid book by law professor Lino A. Graglia (1976).

In the middle phase of desegregation the advocates and opponents perfected and enlarged the scope of their arguments, of course, and the federal courts devised new features and remedial orders on the one hand, and new constraints on remedies on the other. Metropolitan area remedies, for instance, were among the most serious casualties of the middle phase, as in the *Milliken* decision the U.S. Supreme Court devised a rationale for preventing a remedy from going beyond the boundaries of a school district whose liability had already been established by a court. Mandatory student assignments and cross-bussing continued far into the middle phase, but after 1975 the popularity of more voluntary approaches such as magnet schools began to grow tremendously as white political resistance to more comprehensive remedies intensified. Variations on open enrollment, which had picked up a bad name and had been branded a fraud by courts in the way it was used extensively in the South in the early phase, began to make a comeback under new labels. For example, minority-to-majority transfers on a seat-available basis in predominantly white schools became a prime feature of many remedial plans, and courts sanctioned it as acceptable.

As the middle phase waned after 1980, interest in researching and evaluating school desegregation policies and practices waned. The need to conduct more and better large-scale, comparative analyses is as urgent today as it was in 1955, but equity reforms in general faded in political value during the 1980s, and racial desegregation, the capstone of the postmodern era, faded severely as gender and national origin improvements flickered on as educational reform efforts in some states.

WHY FOCUS ON BOSTON?

In the absence of comparative studies, the Boston school desegregation case has some strategic features that make it exceptionally appropriate for case analysis. Only two big city districts more northern than Boston—Minn and Seattle—have done anything to desegregate their schools racially since the *Brown* decision. Minneapolis underwent federal litigation, but its school board voluntarily accepted the finding of liability and asked the court for time in which to develop a truly outstanding remedial plan, which it did. Seattle desegregated voluntarily, without court intervention.

Boston was allegedly a bastion of civil rights and liberties, (Lupo, 1975), although the underseam of racial and nationality group hatreds was as old as the Puritan massacre of Native Americans and as new as the broadcast bigotries of radio talk shows. As the state capital, Boston was the scene in 1850 (Reid, 1978) of the State Supreme Judicial Court decision in the case of Sarah Roberts, whose free African father sought to enroll her in a white public school in Boston. That decision expressed the doctrine of separate but equal, refusing Sarah her opportunity, and the language of the doctrine became almost precisely the language of the U.S. Supreme Court in 1869 in *Plessy v. Ferguson,* which anesthetized the Fourteenth Amendment to the Constitution in race cases until *Brown* in 1954. The Massachusetts legislature outlawed racial segregation in Boston schools in 1855, but the modern legal rationale for it was invented in Boston.

There are other reasons why Boston is strategic for case analysis. Boston is one of the oldest and historically most innovative city school districts in North America. It functioned under laws and other regulations making racial segregation and discrimination unlawful from 1855 until 1965, and in that year state policy in support of racial equity was reaffirmed and made more concrete with the passage of the Racial Imbalance Act. This statute, more progressive than anything of its kind in the other states, designated a public school as unacceptably imbalanced in its student composition if the proportion of "non-white" students exceeded 50 percent, and required state reviewed and approved remedies wherever such imbalances were found.

Boston is also the only school district hosting more than 50,000 students in the entire region composed of the six states of New England, and for the two decades before 1975 it was among the nation's thirty largest public school systems. In addition, the intensity and scope of white resistance toward and defiance of state and federal laws and court orders requiring racial equity were enormous; indeed, they ranked among the North's most violent levels of reaction.

There is one other reason why Boston offers a highly appropriate profile for case study: the city and its public schools have moved on from the heated politics of racial desegregation, a period that extended from 1963 to 1980, and have entered a period of the politics of finance and governance. Thus, enough heat has gone out of the issue to make dispassionate analysis possible.

THE BOSTON CASE OVERALL

The need for a desegregative remedy in Boston was established conclusively between 1963 and 1974 by social scientific research, legal evidence, state agency analyses and policy actions, and, most crucially, by opinions rendered by the Massachusetts Supreme Judicial Court and the U.S. District Court. All of these sources found that students, faculty, and staff were assigned deliberately to schools and to programs within schools by race; that this had been common practice for many decades; that black school facilities, programs, curricula, and materials were inferior to white schools; and that black students were not only transported past white schools close to their homes, but they were also failed, suspended, expelled, and remanded into classes for the mentally retarded and the socially maladjusted at rates three times higher than the rates for white students (*Morgan v. Hennigan*, 1974).

Compounding all of this, school officials and Boston School Committee members pretended that racial segregation and discrimination did not exist or were inadvertent and unintended outcomes of residential segregation.

The federal court devised a permanent remedy early in 1975 because the School Committee submitted to it a constitutionally unacceptable proposal and other parties to the case did the same (Dentler and Scott, 1981). Moreover, the court oversaw implementation of its remedy for fifteen years and issued hundreds of supplementary and modifying orders in that time.

It is doubtful that more than a handful of lawyers, a few dozen educational administrators, and a small band of citizen and child advocates ever read either the court's remedial orders or its later orders, let alone the thousands of pages of legal and expert commentary associated with the case. Sociologist James Coleman, author of the landmark survey of racial segregation in 1966, for example, came to the state to address a joint session of the Massachusetts legislature in 1975 and generalized at length there on the perils of central city school desegregation, but he did not study the record of the case beforehand. Anthony Lukas, Pulitzer prize-winning journalist, spent seven years writing a best-selling account of race relations in Boston, centering on the schools case (1985), but he never studied the court papers or the record of evidence and briefs on which they were based (Dentler, 1986). Some social scientists went so far as to create paranoid interpretations that had little connection with real events: J. Brian Sheehan, for example, an educational anthropologist whose book on the Boston case was published by Columbia University Press, concluded that the federal court remedy was the result of a political cabal between the corporate power structure and the federal judge, a conclusion completely unsubstantiated.

The permanent remedial plan devised and ordered by the federal court (*Morgan v. Kerrigan,* 1975) was an explicit attack on racial exclusion, segregation, and discrimination, as policies and practices maintaining these wrongs had been identified as operating in every domain of public schooling in Boston. Ethnic minorities other than black students were taken into consideration in some parts of the court plan, but because the suit was brought by a group of black parents the plan concentrated primarily on the righting of wrongs done to this group.

There were other substantial boundaries to the plan that grew out of the way the parties had framed the litigation in the first place. The suburbs of Boston were not involved, for example, because they were never named by plaintiffs in the complaint, nor was discovery arranged for the collection of evidence of discrimination in suburban schools. Curriculum, cocurriculum, and instructional matters were not included either, although Judge W. Arthur Garrity, Jr., called for a remedy that "expressed a deep educational concern" (Dentler and Scott, 1981), because they were left untouched by the attorneys for the black parents. Teacher training in preparation for the shift from racially homogeneous to heterogeneous student groups was also not ordered by the court, although the attorney for the Boston Teacher's Union pleaded for its inclusion, because other parties and the judge regarded this as a regular part of the local autonomy due to the School Committee.

The court remedial orders included seven highly substantive domains of the schools and the district, however. Students were assigned to schools and programs such that racially unequal access to them as well as racial isolation of students was ended. In addition to this core of the court plan, teachers and administrators were redistributed and personnel selection was designed so as to raise the level of professional staff from 4 percent to 20 percent black. The administrative structure of the system was reorganized; new and renovated and repaired facilities were ordered, and more than fifty unsafe and unfit buildings were closed; vocational education was redesigned to fit the state's regional system; bilingual instruction was introduced in what became thirteen languages under state and federal laws that had been ignored; special education services were brought into compliance with state and federal laws; and transportation was provided at state expense for desegregation purposes, not merely for distance. Eighteen magnet schools were created. Grade groupings were made virtually uniform citywide. As part of this order, junior high schools were converted into middle schools with grades six through eight and high schools were made into four year comprehensive schools.

SOME SUCCESSES OF THE
FEDERAL COURT PLAN

If we ask if the court plan to achieve racial equity in Boston's public schools was a success or a bungled enterprise, then, we should ask this question from within the actual policy framework of the litigation. This undertaking was no instance of community planning, civic reform politics, or state and local legislation. It was instead a set of federal court orders issued more than a decade after a small group of black parents first asked the Boston School Committee to give a tangible answer to their call for educational improvement and civil rights for their children in the system's schools—a decade marked by the movement led by Dr. Martin Luther King, Jr.—and a call that was answered instead by every conceivable kind of abuse, denial, evasion, and refusal by local and state political leaders. Lukas, for instance, misses the point of this context when he bemoans the absence of a metropolitan area remedy and writes mistakenly as if the federal court could have ordered one (Dentler, 1986).

The primary aim of the court order, the desegregation of students, was achieved, to at least the 85 percent level, between 1975 and 1978, and it has remained constant ever since. The court standard was never, as Nathan Glazer asserted (1972), to hold white students hostage and distribute them widely so that black students could have a chance to sit next to them. Nor was it a standard that presupposed a white student majority. It was rather a standard by which every school would have an enrollment close to the racial/ethnic composition of the subcommunity within Boston from which its students were drawn.

Those who construct the reality of the Boston case as a failure argue that white flight undermined the prospect for authentic desegregation of students. Opponents of desegregation, beginning with School Committee president and later Congresswoman Louise Day Hicks, had long warned that elimination of the neighborhood school and ''forced busing'' would empty Boston of its white children, whose parents would take to suburbs rather than suffer these dangers. Between 1972 when the federal litigation began and 1976 when the permanent remedy had been implemented, white student enrollments declined by half. The warning of Hicks seemed fulfilled.

There was indeed white flight during those years—not to the suburbs, but to Catholic parochial schools and to such cities in the Sunbelt as Phoenix, Tucson, Dallas, Tampa, and Houston. White households had been pouring out of Boston since intense suburbanization began in 1950, and in the 1970s this migration continued but with a change in destination to the states in the South and the West where job opportunities beckoned those caught in a very stagnant New England economy. Black enrollment declined as well, but only slightly because the households were younger and less mobile than white households. Hispanic and Asian enrollments swelled during the 1970s and 1980s, but they constituted a very small fraction of the total population in any event.

The white pill was vastly more influential than white flight in causing white enrollment declines, however. In fact, in the seventy-six suburban public school districts within a twenty-five mile radius of Boston, *white* student enrollments declined by 37.3 percent between 1970 and 1985. In the Boston Public Schools, the *white* enrollments declined by 36.1 percent in the same period. Racial desegregation was certainly not the cause, but birth control and family planning were, as annual live births in the metropolitan area began to decline in 1963 and dropped precipitously from that year through 1975. All but about 6 percent of the white students ''missing'' from the Boston public schools between 1974 and 1985 are in fact students who were never born.

A half dozen racially segregated public schools exist today in Boston. They are located in East Boston, next to Logan Airport, where the court chose to exercise its power to leave them racially isolated because cross-busing would have entailed moving thousands of children two ways daily through the Harbor tunnels, a plan that seemed impractical and educationally undesirable. (Interestingly enough, those once all-white schools have become quite well mixed since 1985 with the arrival into East Boston of many non-black, but ethnic minority, households.) And, there are two or three other schools that fail annually to meet court guidelines. Otherwise, the system is remarkably and peaceably desegregated, and every one of its programs is open fully to students from all racial and ethnic groups. Those who think of racial desegregation in terms of half majority and half minority students or something like this are confused because enrollments in Boston are predominantly minority today.

A second major aim of the court was to desegregate the teaching and administrative staff of the system. When the court case began in 1972 the system's professional personnel were 4 percent black. The court goal of 25 percent has not been achieved to date, but the court-set, short-term standard of 20 percent black and 10 percent other minority was attained by 1984 as a result of nationwide recruitment, opening up a personnel system that was previously composed of more than 90 percent Boston natives drawn overwhelmingly from the Boston Irish ranks of Boston State College. As the schools suffered layoffs from fiscal cutbacks beginning in 1981 and continuing to this day, the court has acted to protect minority staff from being last hired and first fired. The last appeal of this action, subsequent to earlier attempts that failed, was initiated by the Boston Teachers Union and rejected by the U.S. Supreme Court in 1992.

The court not only desegregated the staff; it also reorganized the structure. Some four in ten of the 200 schools lacked building principals in 1974. The court ordered that each building must have a regular full-time principal and that principals and other administrators must be screened and rated by groups of parents and teachers. It ordered the establishment of subdistrict parent and principals' advisory councils and created at headquarters a permanent fifty-two-member department of implementation to execute and monitor the orders.

SPECIAL EDUCATION

The subcase of reforms in special education illustrates how the federal court attempted comprehensive improvements in equity and how these attempts fared (Peters, 1990).

Massachusetts won national fame during the 1960s in its development, passage, and implementation of Chapter 766, the first comprehensive mainstreaming and full-service legislation to transform public special-needs education in this century. That statute became the model for the federal act, PL 94–142. Only Boston among the local districts in Massachusetts ignored and defied Chapter 766. As late as 1974, fewer than 2 percent of all students enrolled in the Boston public schools were receiving special-needs instruction and other services. Assessment and classification procedures were violated at nearly all turns, and staff, facilities, materials, and programs for students with special needs fell far short of state requirements.

The court did not presume to rewrite existing state laws. It referenced these and included an order to the School Committee to comply with them. It also tried to articulate special-needs student assignments with student assignments in general. It ordered that:

> Every school facility shall receive and educate mild and moderate special needs students, who will be assigned to schools in accordance with regular assignment procedures by geocode. No less than one resource room and one special needs services space shall be set aside in each school. Each school shall have special educators and materials. Some moderate and severely handicapped students will be assigned directly to schools with special facilities and staff, apart from the geocode procedure. To support special education both in regular schools and in special resource schools, at least three such special schools in each community district shall be identified and planned by the School Department, for review by representatives of the court . . . No special school shall consist wholly or primarily of special needs students.
>
> (*Morgan v. Kerrigan,* June 1975, Remedial Orders, p. 5)

In other words, special-needs students could be exempt from zoned and cross-busing obligations so long as every subdistrict made full provision to serve them and so long as the desegregation process did not renew conditions that violated the principle of mainstreaming.

There were immediate and generally positive effects as a result of these orders. Most schools in the district had lacked any staff, facilities, or programs, and within one year nearly all had obtained all three. Recruitment of special educators intensified rapidly, and many veteran teachers completed special-needs certification requirements and transferred across into this rapidly expanding sector of the district. There were three times as many students receiving special educational services by 1976 as there had been in 1974.

In spite of progress, Boston remained in extreme noncompliance with state law. The result was *Allen v. McDonough,* the first class action suit brought against a public school district in Massachusetts for violation of Chapter 766 (Rodriguez, 1982). This suit was settled early in 1976, just weeks after it was filed, yet by 1981 Boston had failed to comply with the law (Mass. Advocacy Center, 1978; Walsh, 1980, pp. 193–206), and the suit continued into 1983. Special education enrollment continued to rise rapidly. Indeed, it jumped from 6 percent in 1975 to 16 percent in 1978. In this process, black and hispanic students were extremely overrepresented in retarded, disturbed, and maladjusted categories, while whites were overrepresented in learning disability groups. Maladministration, errors in classification and placement, abrupt dislocations in school and class-room placements for subprograms, and low quality of instructions were among the many grave shortcomings of the district's operations. The power and demands of state law, federal court orders, state judicial decrees, and the efforts of the state education department combined were not sufficient to make special education racially equitable and program-matically effective between 1975 and 1985; gradually, however, very sig-nificant progress toward both objectives was achieved, and the State Board of Education, which had become the monitor for the federal court, recommended termination of the federal orders in this domain a decade after they were issued.

WAS SCHOOL DESEGREGATION BUNGLED?

The subcase of special education shows how court-ordered remedies to advance racial equity may be impeded by circumstances and may take many years to succeed, yet even in this instance as in the major goals of the court, the court plans and their implementation were an indisputable success. One by one, the State Board was able to review the evidence of progress toward full compliance by the Boston public schools in each of the seven major domains, and by 1985 the court was able to withdraw its jurisdiction from nearly all of them on the basis of substantial evidence gathered and analyzed by the state. Some matters were much harder to ac-complish than others, special-education reform among them, but there was no exit for the Boston schools other than compliance, and their attor-neys and key policy makers recognized that as early as 1978.

There were also many very positive, serendipitous effects: Boston School Committee candidates changed, with only occasional throwbacks to tradition, from professional politicians using election in order to move toward higher office over time, to modern civic leaders drawn from the ranks of parents and teachers. Black leaders were elected onto the Com-mittee and the City Council, and hispanic leaders followed. Intergroup relations changed gradually across many racial and ethnic frontiers in the city. Public housing was desegregated, and desegregation of the police force and the fire department accelerated greatly. Above all, election and re-election of mayors became a matter of appealing to all racial and ethnic groups, as opposed to pitting whites against others. As a result, the share of black and other minority groups in public sector power was substantially enlarged by the process of federal court intervention and long-term oversight. The political culture and structure of Boston is very significantly different in 1992 from what it had been when the federal suit was begun in 1972.

Why, then, do so many journalists, educators, and citizens believe school desegregation in Boston was bungled? The files of the *Boston Globe* and the *Boston Herald* alike, for example, are crammed with stories that extend over more than fifteen years that refer uniformly to all aspects of desegregation as if they were parts of a plague or an extended social earthquake that left the city's educational fabric in ruins. In his prize-winning book, Lukas depicted racial violence in parts of Boston during the desegregation years, especially the conflicts inside the old Charlestown High School, with great vividness and tragic themes, but he did not include a section on the emergent new Boston or even its new Charlestown High School.

Most people, based on Lukas's deep and continuous association with the case and the sense this leads him to obtain from countless encounters with student groups, policy makers, journalists, and fellow educators, believe that desegregation plunged the schools into despair and chaos; that they became segregated; teaching and learning declined; services fell apart; costs soared; and parents lost their control over where their children went to school. And, they believe that these gross failures were achieved at the price of terrifying racial violence, race hatred, and the coercive use of force by federal and state officials. The politics of finance and state and regional economic depression have replaced the politics of race and schools in Boston, but the new politics play out against this backdrop of very negative recollections.

A social problem and a social policy solution alike are primarily social constructions of reality (Spector and Kitsuse, 1977; Dentler, 1972). If most people believe strongly, for example, that there is no problem or that the problem is either unimportant to them or is the source of essential advantages, then no solution that is devised to treat it will be construed as worthwhile by the same majority. In addition, no matter how good a policy plan is devised, the same majority will regard it with strong disfavor because it is predicated on introducing substantial changes in order to solve what they regard as a non-problem. And, no disapproval will be more intensely expressed than that aimed, in the final stage of the reality-construction process, at implementation of the new plan.

There is little doubt that a majority of Boston's white citizens regarded racial segregation of the public schools as both nonexistent and a non-problem. Elected officials who declared loudly and repeatedly that segregation did not exist were re-elected with growing margins of the votes. Louise Day Hicks did not stand alone in this regard; rather, she typified the city and state political leadership. If she had not done so, others were pressing eagerly to take her place.

Four in every five white households were sequestered in racial and ethnic enclaves in Charlestown, the North End, Back Bay, Allston and Brighton, East Boston, South Boston, half of Dorchester, Hyde Park, and West Roxbury. Residents of any one of these neighborhoods often knew little about any of the other neighborhoods. The racially mixed neighborhoods of the South End, Roxbury, and Mattapan were the least well-known parts of Boston to the whites from all of the rest of the city.

Racially isolated and 90 to 100 percent black schools were based in the three latter neighborhoods and were of out of sight and mind to nearly all white citizens. What pockets of good schooling existed in the city were lodged, moreover, in Brighton and West Roxbury. Paradoxically, the Latin School and Boston Technical High School, competitive examination schools, were based in black and hispanic neighborhoods, but charter buses were used for decades to transport white students to and from these schools. If racial segregation of the public schools was rejected by the great majority of white voters as a social issue, then school desegregation was unnecessary as well as educationally undesirable.

The federal court plan also had within it a number of serious flaws that impeded and haunted the implementation process for a decade and that helped to reinforce public opposition to the elimination of racial exclusion and the introduction of equity. The plan's rules governing the assignment of students to schools, for example, were too numerous, complex, and technically elaborate to be understood by parents and teachers, and they were hard to carry out administratively as well. Student assignments were mishandled several times in the first years, angering and alienating many politically moderate parents and interest groups in the process. The plan also erred in offering a triple standard for assignments: one for regular schools, one for magnet schools, and another—far less stringent—for the three examination schools. There were other flaws too numerous to catalogue that were minor, but that became exaggerated sources of conflict within the overriding context of resistance to the court orders in general.

The remedial plan ordered by the court was developed in six weeks by four court-appointed masters, two experts, and one special clerk, and the court spent two months thereafter holding hearings on a draft and revising the preliminary proposals. This brief interval cannot begin to compare in quality with what can be achieved by way of problem-solving and planning when it is conducted by the community at large and by ongoing local and state agencies. A court is a last resort for educational problem-solving. It is a poor mechanism through which to develop and perfect educational plans, but when a city's leaders have refused to acknowledge problems or to generate their own solution across many years, a court will intervene.

A court cannot countervail the refusal of public leaders and their followers to acknowledge, let alone deal with, a social problem of racial inequity; its remedial planning efforts will be scarred by the resulting gap between an avoidant polity and itself. Worst of all, a court is poorly situated to carry out a remedial plan. Implementation will, for the most part, take place under the aegis of the defendants who created the problem and maintained it unconstitutionally. As the Boston School Department's court-created office of implementation took up the special-education directives, for example, it became obvious that the office could work on facilities and student assignments to schools, but that the office of special education and the school psychologists were necessarily in charge of screening, diagnosing, classifying, and making individual educational plans for students with special needs, and that these groups were composed of professionals unfamiliar with and indifferent toward the racial desegregation case. They were busy dealing with what they regarded as a completely separate and urgent educational problem of their own. As a result, gross errors were made in 1975 and 1976 in where severely handicapped students were assigned and in faulty changes in those assignments in the second year. Some classes of blind and sight-impaired students, for instance, learned to move about one building for a year, only to be assigned to a different building the next year. At the same time, as court monitors came to examine the records on individual students, they found incomplete workups, missing plans, and complete insensitivity to racial selection questions.

There were other sources of setback and failure in the desegregation process, some of them instances of ironic or perverse and unintended effects of reform. The Boston district based whatever stability and efficacy it had before court intervention upon long-standing and diverse practices of patronage combined with personnel networks built up over long years of shared teaching, administrative, and support services. Custodians kept their jobs because they collected funds for the re-election campaigns of School Committee members. Teachers got tenure and good building assignments because they contributed to those campaigns. Administrators got their appointments by cultivating loyalties to one another in conjunction with reliance upon a patron member of the School Committee or a senior-most administrative officer. As a result, some schools occupied favored positions where they got the best talent and the most resources, thus there was a subsystem of comparatively better schools hidden away inside the larger system of more than 200 schools.

This efficacy was shattered by the parts of the court plan that reorganized the administrative command structure, required open screening and rating of multiethnic candidates for nearly all administrative positions, ended the use of acting principalships, and mandated the recruitment of more than a thousand black, hispanic, and asian educators from outside Boston. This shattering was accompanied by the collapse of old if chaotic record systems, venal payoff and kickback payment schemes, and incompetence of senior staff disguised by trappings of authority. While these had long rendered the district mediocre and riddled with disservice to the public, they had also been the foundations on which communication, mutuality, and cooperative interdependence were built. In the first three years of racial desegregation, delays, errors, and ragged performance at all levels resulted from the breakdown of the old structures and the incompleteness in development of their replacements. Whatever small margins of public tolerance that still persisted after the legal and political disputes of the 1963–1974 period were concluded were sapped by these ironies, and a media and parental image of a gigantic bungle began to take permanent form.

Thus was born the myth, shared by politicians, journalists, school administrators, teachers, and professors alike, that the years from 1974 to 1980 were ones of incredible turbulence, violence, and failure for public education in Boston. Hicks had sketched in the outlines of this myth as early as 1966, but city councilors, state senators and representatives, and elected state officers up to governor came to share in it. Racial desegregation of the public schools would not come to Boston; she had pledged her constituents. But if it did it would ride speedily toward hell in a handbasket of public outrage and system breakdown.

As the reforms took shape, thousands of fearful, angry, and confused white citizens behaved as if both parts of her prophecy had come true. Mayor Kevin White, seeking national political prominence, toured half a dozen cities of the North, for example, with a canned speech declaring that the travesty of Boston's schools should be prevented in other cities wherever and however possible. To this day, both national media and many federal judges and attorneys accept this myth as their theory of the problem with racial desegregation.

One feature of the myth has some validity: teaching and learning, while racially equalized, have not improved to a point where gains in school achievement test scores have occurred. Some of this stems from the absence of mandated curricular and instructional reforms from the court plan. Another part of this stems from the fact that the ranks of relatively advantaged white students have thinned, making the student groups hosted by the Boston school groups in greater need of direct and improved services from school personnel. Most of this, however, is the result of the financial deprivations caused by federal funding disinvestments during the 1980s combined with Massachusetts proposition 21/2. The youngest teachers were the staff most supportive of desegregation, and they were also the most enthusiastic, least burnt-out, classroom instructors. Tragically, most of them were laid off in 1981 and in 1989–1992.

That teaching and learning did not improve significantly was a source of tremendous disappointment for thousands of black parents whose children had borne the brunt of the desegregative process. Their discovery that the quality of learning opportunities in most of the previously white schools were poor and continued to be poor after court intervention led to disillusionment.

Attorney Lawrence Johnson of the Harvard University Law and Education Center, representing the black plaintiffs in the late stages of the litigation, proposed to the court an exchange of parts of the desegregative remedies in exchange for improvements in teaching and support services and increased shares of power in the system for black leaders. This proposal was carried into the federal district court in the form of a proposal for freedom of choice by Johnson in 1984. The court held hearings and then rejected the proposal, but its self-styled ''final order'' of 1985 (in fact there were subsequent orders) permitted the School Committee to change student assignment policies in order to increase freedom of choice, so long as the results remained fully desegregative. In 1989, the Committee adopted a controlled choice plan similar to those already in use in other Massachusetts cities such as Cambridge.

This modification did not affect levels of student achievement, however. As the politics of finance overtook and obliterated the issue of racial equity in the 1989–1992 period, moreover, accountability for the performance of the district became such a flaming question in Boston as to lead to dissolution of the School Committee and creation of an alternative board appointed by the mayor.

CONCLUSION

The racial desegregation process in the Boston public schools thus not only attacked racial and ethnic exclusion and the long-standing ravages of discrimination, but succeeded in eliminating most of the historic policies and practices that had been wittingly used to preserve it. Vast changes were effected as a result of federal court intervention, orders, and the exercise of oversight across a period of fifteen years. Most of the changes were carried out peacefully and effectively in most schools during the first five years of the process, though six schools and the neighborhoods around them—most notably South Boston—became staging areas for protest, defiance, and violent confrontations generated by white opponents.

The turbulence and violence resulting from these few events were widely sanctioned by city and state political leaders and were covered firsthand in South Boston by hundreds of journalists from around the world. In the course of the three years between 1974 and 1976, these side-pocket events reified the national myth that school racial desegregation was a terrible process to undergo and that justice itself had been botched in Boston.

The court remedies made racial isolation unlawful, closed unfit and dungeon-like buildings, offered magnet school opportunities to one in every three students in the system, brought into being a special-education service subsystem for the first time in the history of the city, introduced a much improved and enlarged bilingual subsystem, caused the construction of new and renovated facilities, increased federal and state investments, created partnerships with colleges, businesses, and cultural agencies that became models emulated nationwide, and, above all, modified race relations and the politics of ethnic relations throughout the region in the direction of improved harmony and power-sharing.

For all of these profound successes, the myth that desegregation failed badly in Boston supports the ethnic, gender, and socioeconomic stratification arrangements (Persell, 1977) that have been embedded in American educational thinking for a century.

REFERENCES

Boardman, R. P. 1971. "A Comparison of the Academic Performance and Achievement of Fifth and Sixth Grade Pupils in a Program of Pupil Transfer," Ph.D. diss. Columbia University Teachers College.

Coleman, J. S., et al. 1966. *Equality of Educational Opportunity.* Washington, D.C.: GPO.

Dentler, R. A. 1972. *Major Social Problems.* Chicago: Rand McNally.

Dentler, R. A., and B. M., and M. E. Warschauer. 1967. *The Urban R's: The Problem of Race Relations in Urban Education.* New York: Frederick Praeger.

———. 1986. "The Fallowness of Common Ground," *New England Journal of Public Policy* 2,1 no. 1, pp. 81–102.

Dentler, R. A., and M. B. Scott. 1981. *Schools on Trial.* Cambridge, MA: Abt Books.

Glazer, N. "Is Busing Necessary?" *Commentary* 53: pp. 39–52.

Graglia, L. A. 1976. *Disaster by Decree: The Supreme Court Decisions on Race and the Schools.* Ithaca: Cornell University Press.

Hawley, W., ed. 1981. *Assessment of Current Knowledge About the Effectiveness of School Desegregation Strategies.* vols. 1–7 Nashville: Center for Education and Human Development Policy.

Kirp, D. L. 1982. *Just Schools: The Idea of Racial Equality in American Education.* Berkeley: University of California Press.

Kluger, R. 1976. *Simple Justice.* New York: Knopf.

Lupo, A. 1977. *Liberty's Chosen Home: The Politics of Violence in Boston.* Boston: Little, Brown.

Lukas, J. A. 1985. *Common Ground.* New York: Knopf.

Massachusetts Advocacy Center. 1978. *Double Jeopardy: The Plight of Minority Students in Special Education.* Boston.

Miller, N., and M. B. Brewer. 1984. *Groups in Contact: The Psychology of Desegregation.* New York: Academic Press.

Orfield, G. 1978. *Must we bus? Segregated schools and national policy.* Washington, D.C.: Brookings.

Persell, H. 1977. *Education and inequality.* New York: Free Press.

Peters, S. 1990. "Mainstreaming and integration of exceptional children: A sociological perspective." In *Readings on Equal Education.* ed. S. S. Goldberg. Vol. 10, New York: AMS Press. 169–92.

Raffel, J. 1980. *The politics of school desegregation.* Philadelphia: Temple University Press.

Reid, A. G. 1978. *The Sarah Roberts case of 1849.* Boston: WGBH Educational Foundation.

Rodriguez, A. 1982. *Special education in Boston: Court monitor's report.* Boston: Suffolk Superior Court.

St. John, N. 1975. *Desegregation.* New York: John Wiley.

Sheehan, J. B. 1984. *The Boston school integration dispute.* New York: Coumbia University Press.

Spector, M., and J. Kitsuse. 1977. *Constructing social problems.* Menlo Park, CA: Cummings.

Walsh, C. E. 1980. *Yearbook of equal education in Massachusetts.* Amherst, MA: Horace Mann Bond Center. 193–206.

Weinberg, M. 1970. *Desegretation research: An appraisal.* 2d ed. Bloomington, IN: Phi Delta Kappa.

Willie, C. V. 1982. *School desegregation plans that work.* Westport, CT: Greenwood Press.

Wolters, R. 1984. *The burden of Brown: Thirty years of school desegregation.* Nashville: University of Tennessee Press.

EDUCATION VOUCHERS AND DESEGREGATION PROGRAMS:
PROSPECTS AND REMEDIES

Ronald G. Corwin and Robert Dentler

School desegregation is a process and a goal under which no student is denied access to a school, or program, or treated unfavorably or isolated or separated in any way because of race, gender, or national origin. Desegregation plans may also include program enrichments, service improvements, or special support for formerly segregated students in process of being helped to overcome the affects of past discrimination.

We are concerned about the possibility that education voucher plans will set back thirty years of effort to desegregate schools in this country. As we will use the term, a voucher plan is one that permits parents to use public money to send their children to private schools. We identify some potential problems and offer possible remedies.

THE MYTHS OF PRIVATIZATION

The case for privatization with respect to education through vouchers thrives on at least three myths: (1) competition from the private sector will create segmented markets with many different types of schools providing for every need; (2) public bureaucracies are unnecessary and wasteful;

and (3) better schools, producing smarter kids, will be propagated by free enterprise and nurtured by concerned parents.

The argument, in profile, is that public schools are being choked by rules and red tape and an army of expendable autocrats. The public school monopoly has become unaccountable to concerned parents and inaccessible to creative teachers. Competition from private schools will jolt the public sector back to life. They will either change or go under. Advocates of privatization claim that private schools not only are more effectively organized, but also produce smarter kids than the public sector.

THE ISSUES

The Free Market Fantasy

The market model fits neither education, as it operates in this country, nor the voucher plans that have been thus far designed. It does not apply to education, since education is a public good, not a private good. Durkheim was one of the first scholars to advocate public control over education because schools are the principal sources of common societal values, which are prerequisite to the social integration of complex societies. It is commonly recognized that schools in the United States have helped to assimilate large immigrant populations by mixing children from diverse backgrounds within classrooms (Levin, 1983). If parents choose their own schools, however, and if schools can select students, they will then be free to seek out exclusive settings embracing children of the same backgrounds.

The market model does not apply to education voucher plans because politicians, not parents, make the fundamental choices. A voucher is a form of subsidy. Its amount is set by politicians, not by the market. It is the value of the voucher, not the free market, that predetermines which schools survive, which will not. If the full tuition and travel are covered, vouchers could open doors for the poor to any school that wants them, but when vouchers fall short of the full cost, they not only fail to help the poor; but they also subsidize the wealthy who can afford to pay the difference. Thus, the fate of the poor and of the schools themselves hinges on politics, not markets. The real issue, then, is choice for whom? At least some choices will be reserved for the few.

Bureaucracy As Villain

Public schools are being denounced as top-down and rule-driven oligarchies, more sensitive to government bodies that provide funds, labor unions, and special-interest groups than to parents with children in school.

The leading proponents of vouchers maintain that effective schools must have freedom to develop their own programs. They believe the private sector provides the necessary autonomy (Chubb and Moe, 1990; Coons and Sugarman, 1992).

We would argue, on the contrary, that the problem is sometimes too little bureaucracy, rather than too much. Throwing out rules and standards designed to provide equitable protection of the public interest will only increase the opportunities for special interests and authorities to act capriciously. The purpose of bureaucracy is precisely to insulate public employees from personalized forms of power and special interests (Weber, 1947).

The Quality Question

Studies based on a sample of eighty-four Catholic schools reveal that, compared to their public school counterparts, Catholic students average less than a grade higher on standardized reading and math tests (Coleman and Hoffer, 1987). However, private school students are screened based on their academic performance and conduct. They have displayed ability and fewer problems. For example, students who have language difficulties or who need special services seldom enroll in private schools.

IMPLICATIONS FOR DESEGREGATION

Extrapolating from the myths and underlying issues identified, we believe it is likely that education vouchers will aggravate the segregation problem in at least three ways, namely by increasing the political disadvantage of minorities, segregating academically superior students, and diverting attention and resources from other alternatives for desegregating and otherwise improving schools.

Political Disadvantage and
Desegregation

If voucher plans are governed by the political arena, the consequences are predicated on political power, in combination with market mechanisms. Given the bargaining disadvantage of poor minorities, is it likely they will be the prime beneficiaries of a politically driven voucher system? In economics, "demand" is worthless unless the customer can pay for desired goods and services. Even with a voucher, many low-income students will be unable to pay for transportation, books, and fees. Moreover, vouchers do not cover the costs of expensive special services. Presently, most private schools do not offer special programs for students with educational or physical handicaps, or with language deficiencies. Without special provisions and compensation, these programs will not materialize. Also, many private schools, including some Catholic schools, are located in middle-income suburbs that often are not receptive to minorities.

Skimming and Desegregation

Schools and parents have mutual interests in keeping private schools selective. On the one hand, private schools occupy a special niche in the market precisely because they are selective and can skim the most desirable students; the public schools take the rest.[1] Catholic schools attract and select students suited to their academic programs, thus creaming off some of the best students from the public sector. Catholic schools do enroll high percentages of minority students, but the pattern of selectivity suggests that they, too, are a handpicked group.

On the other hand, parents who prefer private schools may be looking for more than an academic setting. Some are being pushed out by social problems associated with many public schools today. Others are undoubtedly being pulled by the attraction of exclusive communities of students and parents who share the same religious, political, and social backgrounds. This quest for homogeneity contradicts the larger societal objective of reducing racial, social, and cultural isolation.

Fragmentation and Desegregation

Voucher programs are thus piecemeal solutions to holistic problems. They divert attention and resources from the issue of desegregation and create still other problems. Most private schools today are responding to only one type of demand, the demand for academic programs for problem-free students. There are no equally viable counterpart movements pushing for schools designed to cope with other educational needs—the needs of economically, culturally, and educationally handicapped kids, the ones with physical and cultural handicaps, those who need remedial help, those with behavioral and drug problems, the ones with babies, the ones who cannot speak English; in short, the ones private schools do not want. In this sense, privatization is a piecemeal approach to the fundamental problems facing education. The solution, we think, has less to do with privatization than with finding alternatives for those kids private schools do not serve.

CHOICE AS A DIVISION OF LABOR PROBLEM

Desegregation policies of the federal courts and state school boards are guided by the principles of the Civil Rights Act. They regulate equity issues of all kinds. Thus, racial, gender, and national origin equity questions take the desegregation process into the heartland of curricular and instructional specialization and adaptations necessary to deliver special services. Desegregation today, therefore, pertains to bilingual and ESL instruction; student safety and discipline; multicultural instruction; and policies to eliminate gender segregation in work study, cooperative, and vocational instruction, to mention only a few areas. These special provisions have become increasingly essential, and they are absent from most private schools.

The programs and practices just mentioned provide a few narrow choices that are not readily available to many students. Of schools in the private sector, only a minuscule percentage focus on special education and learning alternatives. The overwhelming majority emphasize one alternative, academics. Other alternatives are needed in the public and private sectors.

Obsolescence of the Common School

In short, for most parents, the only realistic prospect is the traditional common school. The private school choice movement has an appeal for many parents because many common schools are not working, and they are looking for alternatives. Common schools use an embryonic division of labor out of step with the requirements of a technocratic society. Once regarded as the first line of defense against elitism, some common schools have become as obsolete as the general store.[2]

Remedies

We propose two approaches to cope with the potential problems we have been discussing: legislation and controlled choice. The first approach is to lobby for legislation to govern any school that redeems a voucher paid for by public money. Since the voucher is a public subsidy, it should be governed by law. The same laws and interpretations that apply to the public sector, with respect to desegregation requirements, should apply to voucher programs. This would mean establishing rules governing admissions practices, promotion and discipline policies, curriculum tracking, and the like.

Controlled choice is another tack related to the legislative approach. This term has been used by several experts in desegregation. It refers to a modified choice strategy under which parents may apply to more than one school, acceptance being subject to controls for racial/ethnic composition and openings (Dentler, 1991).

The second approach is to attack the underlying reasons that are driving parents to search out alternatives to public schools. We maintain that a central problem, which accounts for many others, is that there are too few planned alternatives in the public sector from which parents may choose. The remedy we propose is a comprehensive system of specialized schools designed to provide comprehensive services to meet the needs of most students while simultaneously fostering desegregation goals.

Desegregation and Special Education Services

There is a ubiquitous tension between the goal of desegregation in our complex society and the growing demand for specialized facilities to provide services to all children at risk. With respect to human services, specialization requires segregating different clienteles into specially equipped and staffed settings where their problems can be treated by trained personnel. A heart hospital is a clear example. We see three ways of coping with the tension between desegregation and specialization.

First, some desegregation programs focus on mixing students from varied social backgrounds without much regard for their special needs. This is the philosophy behind the common school, which we have already discussed.

Second, some desegregation programs cope with the tension by setting up magnet schools. Typically, they specialize along curricular lines: the arts; sciences, mathematics and computers; social studies occupations, such as health care; general academics, such as college preparation and honors courses; and traditional and fundamental schools.

Programs linking urban-to-suburban and minority-to-majority districts, like magnet school choice, are analogous to school vouchers, except that the former entail political controls to prevent the rejection of some minority applicants. Such controls shape the general composition (racial, national origin, and gender) of each sending and receiving school. Without them, resegregation is always accelerated.

Most large school districts have alternative or magnet schools of some type. However, few students thus far attend such schools. For example, 200 of the 15,000 school districts in the U.S. have magnet school programs. Of 70,000 schools, 1,500 are magnet schools. Nevertheless, extensive growth of magnet schools is foreseeable. Dentler observes that "The evidence is solid that, nationwide, practitioners know how to develop and maintain racially and ethnically desegregated magnet schools'' (Dentler, 1991:8).

The magnet school idea can serve as a linchpin for the third option, the one we advocate, namely a *system of specialized schools*. The system we have in mind would not be limited to academic alternatives. It must be planned to provide a full range of *social* services. The personal dimension, the source of legion problems and pathologies that afflict schools today has been neglected in the organizational structure of public school districts. Social services might include:

1. School-based health care facilities for drug problems, pregnancy, and sexually transmitted diseases, and day care
2. Counseling and diagnostic centers for students who have been affected by violence, vandalism, and verbal or sexual harassment; for recent immigrants; and for students returning to classes after jail sentences or extended truancy
3. Language clinics for LEP students
4. Remedial schools and programs for students with educational and learning deficiencies
5. Teacher centers focused on helping teachers learn to cope with specific problems (such as a deaf child or a child who cannot speak English).

A Systemic Approach to
Specialization

Some types of specialized schools, of course, have been around a long time—vocational schools and schools devoted to special education, the arts, and to modern technologies. However, while they exist, these schools are not prevalent in the public sector. Moreover, they are even more rare in the private sector. Only 12 percent of private schools in the United States are dedicated to special education students (National Center for Educational Statistics, 1991:3).

We want to underscore that we are not talking about some isolated special schools. Instead, we advocate that states and their public school districts should plan an entire system of specialized schools to operate alongside common schools. There must be enough options, for all kinds of children, to provide meaningful alternatives to the common school that meet a full spectrum of needs. In other words, each specialized organizational unit (e.g., a school or a classroom) must take its place as a planned alternative within a systematic division of labor.

The concept of a division of labor is double-edged. On the one hand, each unit (whether school, classroom, or program) has a particular focus

ular focus and competency, and it is staffed by skilled workers trained to perform interdependent roles required to carry out the program objectives. The staff must be well trained and supported by a structure comprising (1) interdependent professionals, and paraprofessionals, whose roles are clearly defined, (2) an evaluation and incentive system, (3) governance and appeal mechanisms, and (4) linkages to parents and other schools and service agencies in and outside the district. All of the pieces must be present. For example, holding teachers accountable for outcomes cannot be justified if the other forms of support are absent.

On the other hand, the different units making up the alternatives have meaning only in relation to each other. One must understand the total system of relationships to assess the value of a given alternative. Systemic specialization is planned, comprehensive, balanced, and equitable. To form a systemic division of labor, one links objectives, which have been identified for different types of students, to their condition and then establishes appropriate organizational structures. Objectives may be academic, social, vocational, or religious. The condition of students refers to whether they are motivated or alienated, idealistic or pragmatic, well prepared or not. Some have personal problems (drugs), handicaps (language deficiency), or conflicting responsibilities (a baby).

The division-of-labor question asks if alternatives are available to meet such needs. Every school specializes in some way to accomplish different things. When the system is viewed as a whole, the gaps and the redundancies will become apparent.[3]

Specialization makes it possible to specify clearly for each school what it is expected to produce. This has two important consequences. *First,* unless the product is identified, no one—not the school board, administrators, teachers, or students—can be held accountable for anything beyond attendance and literacy. But, when specialized competency is made explicit, sanctions and rewards can be tied to the performances of each official, teacher, and student. *Second,* when the product is clearly differentiated, competitive relationships between winners and losers are transformed into compatible relationships among providers.

CONCLUSIONS

The education-voucher movement is a circumscribed reform targeted for as yet few parents who are seeking safe and tranquil, culturally homogenous academic environments. Vouchers are likely to aggravate the segregation problem in at least three ways: by increasing the political disadvantage of minorities, by segregating academically superior students, and by diverting attention and resources from other alternatives for desegregating and otherwise improving schools. We propose two approaches to cope with these potential problems.

First, both legislative and controlled-choice approaches are needed to govern any school that redeems a voucher paid for by public money. Second, the remedy we proposed here is a system of specialized schools designed to provide comprehensive services to meet the needs of most students. Specialization has not reached its potential within public education. We argue that, to achieve equity, specialized programs must be linked to students' social backgrounds and concerns. For example, racially diverse districts could set up ongoing programs dealing with discrimination, hate crimes, and gangs. Schools could be established to work with students of a given national origin needing help with language or adjusting to a new culture, or various cultural and racial groups can be mixed in programs focusing on cultural values, life styles, or generic minority problems. Other centers could be established concerned with gender issues, such as sex equity or sexual harassment.

Something like magnet schools can serve as base schools designed to provide social services, besides curricular alternatives. Teachers would be trained to carry out the focal theme of the school, whether remedial work, bilingual teaching, or high-risk students, such as potential drop outs or teenage mothers. These schools would work collaboratively with other satellites (schools, centers, programs, and public and private agencies and programs) to provide specialized services for students in need. Students could enter schools either by being assigned by the district or by controlled choice of parents.

Mechanisms needed to create a systemic division of labor, which can serve the full spectrum of youths in school today, already exist, yet, still others need to be invented.[4] We have in mind mechanisms like joint programs and centers established in collaboration among schools, districts, and service agencies in *both* the public and private sectors; desegregated home (or base) schools; flexible scheduling, including evening, weekend, summer, and alternate-day rotating schedules; short or mini courses; and bussing.

Ronald Corwin is Professor of Sociology, The Ohio State University. Robert Dentler is Emeritus Professor of Sociology, University of Massachusetts and is an authority on school desegregation.

This discussion draws freely from companion papers published by Southwest Regional Laboratory. See Dentler, 1991; Dianda and Corwin, 1992; and Corwin, 1992.

NOTES

1. The extent of skimming is suggested in a national study of private schools based on information from 1987. Most Catholic high schools require for admission a standardized achievement or aptitude test (77 percent) or a test developed by the school (22 percent), a strong academic record (61 percent), recommendations of elementary school principals (73 percent), and successful completion of the previous year (98 percent); also, about half require interviews with parents and students. Catholic high schools generally do not serve special-education students. Only a few private schools provide bilingual services (9 percent), English as a second language (12 percent), programs for the handicapped (18 percent), and vocational/technical programs (14 percent). They are more inclined to provide academic services such as remedial reading (69 percent), remedial mathematics (53 percent), foreign languages (46 percent), and programs for the gifted and talented (33 percent).

2. For some good news about thousands of today's public schools, however, see J. Schneider, in press, *Excellence and equity.*

3. An effective division of labor must be integrated into the basic structure of the school and school district. Grouping and tracking typically do not meet this criterion. They may seem to be forms of specialization because they bring together students with similar social backgrounds. However, they are not supported by incentives, structures, and the kind of staffing needed to target expertise most effectively. Both grouping and tracking are afterthoughts added to structures designed for other purposes. In practice, tracking often amounts to a de facto form of skimming, a vehicle for diverting expertise to the accelerated track. Therefore, grouping and tracking experiences are not tests of the feasibility of within school specialization.

4. Similarly, most of what we propose now exists. However, we are addressing the issue of institutionalizing them by establishing permanent facilities and organizational units and creating the necessary systemic linkages. Many of the programs and facilities can be shared among school districts within a region or metropolitan area. Others can be subcontracted with schools and service agencies in the private sector.

REFERENCES

Brigham, F. H. 1992. *Catholic elementary and secondary schools, 1991–92.* National Catholic Education Association.

Chubb, J. E. and T. M. Moe. 1990. *Politics, markets, and America's schools* Washington, D.C.: Brookings Institution.

Coleman, J. S. and T. Hoffer. 1987. *Public and private high schools.* New York: Basic Books.

Coons, J. E. and S. D. Superman. 1992. *Scholarships for children.* Berkeley CA: Institute of Governmental Studies Press; University of California.

Corwin, R. G. *Can vouchers reform public education?* SWRL Occasional Paper Series. Los Alamitos, CA: Southwest Regional Laboratory. Forthcoming.

Dentler, R. *The national evidence on magnet schools.* SWRL Occasional Paper Series. Los Alamitos, CA: Southwest Regional Laboratory, 1991.

Dianda, M. and R. G. Corwin. *What a voucher can buy: A survey of California's private schools.* Los Alamitos, CA: Southwest Regional Laboratory, 1992 (In Press).

Durkheim, E. (rptd. 1961). *Moral education.* Glencoe. The Free Press.

Levin, H. M. 1983. "Educational choice and the pains of democracy." pp. 17–38 in *Public dollars for private schools: The case of tuition tax credits,* Philadelphia, PA: Temple University Press. 17–38.

National Center for Educational Statistics. 1991. *Private schools in the United States: A statistical profile, with comparisons to the public schools.* Washington, D.C.: U.S. Department of Education.

Robinson, G. E. and N. J. Protheroe. 1987. *Cost of education: An investment in America's future.* Arlington, VA: Educational Research Service.

Schneider, J. "Excellence and Equity." In Press, 1992.

Weber, M. 1947. *The theory of social and economic organization.* A. M. Henderson and T. Parsons (Trans.) New York: Oxford University Press.

DUE PROCESS RIGHTS
OF STUDENTS:
THE IMPACT OF *GOSS* TODAY

Tedi K. Mitchell

HISTORICAL BACKGROUND

Although the issue of the due process rights of students had been the topic of both print discussion and court litigation for many years, it gained greater prominence after the United States Supreme Court decided *In re Gaul* in 1967.[1] This decision stated that young people under the care of the juvenile justice system were entitled to procedural due process. The *Gault* holding enabled legal scholars to argue the case for student due process rights with renewed vigor. Litigation addressing the question of whether or not students were entitled to due process before they were suspended or expelled from school also increased. The answer to that question varied, however, depending upon the federal circuit and the circumstances of the individual case. While the majority of the decisions were concerned with long-term suspensions and expulsions, there were some that addressed the issue of short-term suspensions. In these cases, also, the courts were divided in their opinions about the need for due process. In *Linwood v. Board of Education, City of Peoria, Schools District No. 150, Ill.* (1972), for example, the Seventh Circuit Court of Appeals ruled that a short-term suspension (in this case, seven days or less) was "a minor disciplinary

53

penalty which the legislature may elect to treat differently from expulsion or prolonged suspension without violating a constitutional right of the student.''[2] As far as a hearing requirement was concerned, the court concluded that ''it was within the discretion of the lawmakers to equate suspension of 7 days or less with other minor disciplinary penalties.''[3] In *Vail v. Board of Education of Portmouth School District* (1973), however, a New Hampshire federal district court ruled that any suspension requires minimal due process procedures—specifically, an informal consultation with the student prior to suspension.[4] At that time the student should be told why he is suspended, be allowed to tell his side of the story, and be given an opportunity to persuade the administrator that the disciplinary action is not justified. The Supreme Court would resolve the problem when it ruled on still another short-term suspension case, *Goss v. Lopez* (1975).[5]

In 1973, *Lopez v. Williams,* a class-action suit was heard by a three-judge district court in the southern district of Ohio, Eastern Division.[6] Two years earlier, during February and March 1971, a very large group of students (seventy-six from one school alone) were suspended from the junior and senior high schools of Columbus. The Ohio education code permitted student suspensions for up to ten days without a prior hearing, but it required administrators to notify a disciplined student's parent or guardian within twenty-four hours after the fact and, further, to state the reasons for taking such disciplinary action. The principals failed to do so, never contacting parents in some instances. The students sought a declaration stating that the above code section was unconstitutional because ''it permitted public school administrators to deprive plaintiffs of their right to an education without a hearing of any kind in violation of the procedural due process component of the Fourteenth Amendment.''[7] The court upheld the students, and the school district's appeal went directly to the Supreme Court. An out-of-court settlement was never attempted because school board members and officials ''would not give an inch in admitting that their autonomy might be limited by constitutional requirements.''[8] They ''were not going to give up until the United States Supreme Court told them they were wrong.[9] The Court had been asked to decide whether or not students had a right to due process before being suspended from school. Specifically, was a student facing a short-term suspension (ten days or less) entitled to some form of procedural due process? Oral arguments were heard in 1974 and on 22 January 1975 the Court handed down its decision.

THE SUPREME COURT HANDS DOWN *GOSS*

The Supreme Court declared in *Goss v. Lopez* that all students facing suspension ''must be given some kind of notice and afforded some kind of hearing'' before being suspended unless the student's presence ''poses a continuing danger to persons or property or an ongoing threat of disrupting the academic process.'' [10] Due process procedures must follow as soon as it is practical if a student is removed immediately. Students facing longer suspensions and expulsions probably require more formal procedures, but the Court did not specify what they were. Moreover, there might be some ''unusual situations'' even when it comes to short suspensions that would require more than the ''rudimentary procedures.'' The Court stated that they did not believe they had ''imposed procedures on school disciplinarians'' that were ''inappropriate in a classroom setting'' because one of the Columbus principals had testified that his school ''had an informal procedure, remarkably similar to that which we now require applicable to suspensions generally but which was not followed in this case.'' [11] They also noted that Columbus school principals ''are now required by local rule to provide at least as much as the constitutional minimum which we have described.'' [12]

EDUCATIONAL AND LEGAL RESPONSES TO *GOSS*

The reactions to *Goss* revealed strong disagreement within the educational and legal communities regarding this decision and its impact on education in the future. The National Education Association's president supported the decision, while the American Federation of Teachers' president asserted that the ruling would create more problems for the schools. The *New York Times* reported that school administrators, in general, seemed ''to agree with the principle of due process,'' but a number of them feared the ruling would ''further weaken the principal's hand in dealing with severe disciplinary problems in urban schools.'' [13] Local and state officials were interviewed, and many felt their state regulations were already in compliance with *Goss.*

Twenty-eight law journals reviewed the decision within a year after it was handed down. The majority of commentators believed the doctrine of *in loco parentis* had been dealt a fatal blow but that the Court's due process requirement would not overburden the schools because ''*Goss* imposes standards defined more by common sense than by technical legal criteria.'' [14] Some had doubts about the impact, however, either because school officials were already doing what *Goss* mandated or administrators would only give lip service to the procedure. On reviewer noted that while Montana's legislature had required school trustees to define suspension and expulsion procedures as early as 1971, there were still districts that had no

formal discipline policies in 1975. Moreover, there were significant differences in the policies adopted by the various boards.[15] This was also true
in other states that neither required a uniform state-wide policy, or monitored the policies adopted at the local level.

Similar opinions were also articulated by a group of thirty experts from
law and education who were brought together by the National Institute of
Education in April 1975 to discuss the Court's student rights decisions.
Some of the participants' commentaries were published by the *Journal of
Law and Education* (October 1975), which devoted the entire issue to examining the implications of *Goss* and *Wood v. Strickland,* a decision handed
down in February of the same year.[16]

William Buss, a University of Iowa law professor, who had written a
treatise on student due process in 1971, thought that there were four possible responses to the decision by school officials. First, "*Goss* may simply
be ignored, out of ignorance or lawlessness or both."[17] He noted that
judicial impact studies that examined responses to the prayer and Bible
reading decisions revealed "that values people place higher than confor-
mity to Supreme Court opinions have guided action in many, many school
districts . . . that the gap between law declaration and law implementation
is often cavernous."[18] Second, as was already mentioned in the law
reviews, school administrators could respond with "technical compliance
without any real change of substance," following the procedure "without
any intention to take seriously the student's response, or in practice, without ever finding the student's response consequential," the teacher's side
of the controversy always being accepted.[19] Third, some school officials
might avoid "discipline in order to avoid the jeopardy of non-compliance"
simply because they may be "intimidated by *Goss* requirements."[20] And,
fourth, school officials might respond to the spirit of *Goss*. Students, in
turn, would see the legal system working and prompt, open-minded treatment would "reinforce the several levels of behavior being questioned or
affected."[21]

Alan Levine, an attorney for the New York American Civil Liberties
Union, concluded that the impact of *Goss* would be minimal. "Some
schools will become fairer than they were," but the required hearing
would be "a mere formality to a school administrator determined to suspend a student."[22]

Arthur Kola, an Ohio attorney whose firm provided counsel to school
boards and had filed an amicus brief on behalf of the defendant administrators, thought that numerous lawsuits would follow attempting "to
build, at the very least, on the 'unusual situations' exception" mentioned
by the Court. Further, suits would also be pressed "to extend the due

process concept beyond suspensions and expulsions to other routine school decisions.''[23]

William Hazard, a professor of education, concluded that school people needed to be better informed about students' constitutional rights, and pre-service and in-service training programs should be developed to disseminate this information. He also believed that there might be a renewed effort to find legally acceptable alternatives to suspension procedures, that ''current procedures generally are defended for their management value and few educators claim any substantial educational benefit to the . . . student.'' While the presence of some students truly threatens both the educational mission and safety of others, ''suspensions . . . are little more than admissions of failure by the school and the community.''[24]

Comments about the decision by the staff of the Center for Law and Education, which argued the students' case before the Supreme Court, were published in *Inequality In Education* (July 1975). Paul Weckstein, a research assistant, was primarily concerned with expanding the impact of *Goss* on life within the school. He argued that some procedural protection might be applicable before making decisions about academic evaluation, exclusion from extracurricular activities, involuntary transfers, placement in special classes or schools, tracking, challenging student records, corporal punishment, the administration of behavior modifying drugs, limitations on freedom of expression, and exclusion for ''medical'' reasons.[25]

Two other educators, Chester Nolte and Ronald Anson, also reviewed the decision. Nolte, a former school superintendent, stated that local boards should ''assert their domination in the area of ensuring student rights because if they did not act students would ''continue to press upward . . . for redress of grievances'' not remedied at the local level.[26] Legislatures and/or state boards of education, as well as the courts, would then be asked to define student rights policies and local decision-making authority would be further curtailed. Anson, a National Institute of Education staff member, thought it unlikely that the lower courts would add further proceduralization and extend *Goss* beyond its limits because that was ''the very thing Supreme Court inveighed against.''[27]

Sixteen years have passed since these educational and legal scholars voiced their opinions concerning the possible consequences of *Goss* on the management and operation of public schools. Their commentaries raise four questions that this chapter attempts to answer. The first asks if state decision-makers responded to *Goss* and enacted statutory and/or administrative regulations requiring procedural due process before suspending a student for ten days or less. The second concerns the response of the judiciary. Have the decisions handed down since *Goss* further expanded the impact of *Goss* on life within the schools, and, if they have, in what areas? The third area of inquiry concerns the use of disciplinary alternatives to suspension. The literature on this topic will be used to ascertain if alternatives have been developed and then the kinds of alternatives and their usage by school districts. The final question probes the behavior of local school district administrators. Buss, Levine, and Hazard each posed possible responses by local educators that now can be explored and examined. To accomplish this task, we studied school site administrators' attitudes and responses to discipline in four southern California school districts; the results are reported in the fourth section of this chapter.

STATE STATUTORY AND
REGULATORY RESPONSE TO *GOSS*

The *Goss* decision sanctioned the behavior of appellant school officials and those similarly situated. Buss noted that these implementors might ignore the decision either because of lack of knowledge or, as the judicial impact studies have revealed, because they did not agree with it, their actions being guided by a different set of values. A study of due process procedures in Indiana's public schools conducted about seven years after *Goss* was handed down, however, provided a very important finding. When asked whether or not the Supreme Court had ever decided a case dealing with public school suspension procedures, only 70.6 percent of the administrators knew about *Goss,* and, of that percentage, only 41 percent disclosed accurate knowledge about what the decision requires. Because the state legislature had enacted legislation that complied with procedural requirements of *Goss,* however, the overwhelming majority of administrators (94 percent) knew that students were entitled to due process before they could be suspended from school (except in emergency situations).[28] Since state legislatures (and state boards of education that have been delegated generalized rule-making authority) have ultimate authority over education, the most logical way to ensure both knowledge, uniformity, and compliance at the local level is to enact statutory or administrative regulations at the state level.

A review of the fifty state education codes and administrative regulations revealed that, as of February 1992, thirty-three states have enacted procedural due process provisions for students facing short-term suspensions that comply with the *Goss* decision. Four additional states provide post-suspension due process. Table 1 reflects some of the findings of this review.

Further analysis of the statutes and regulations provides additional information. The state boards of education of Alaska and Delaware require their departments of education to review local school board disciplinary policies. The Arkansas State Board requires the Department of Education to monitor school district compliance. Georgia's Education Code defines short-term and long-term suspensions and expulsions, but no short-term procedures are given. Illinois and Mississippi codes require that parents/ guardians be notified of their student's suspension, but a post-suspension hearing is optional, held only if the parent/guardian requests it.[29] Although the Texas Education Code does not explicitly state that students are to be given notice and a hearing before suspension, the statute does require the principal to investigate the incident before suspending a student. And the state board's administrative regulations require districts to have a management plan that sets forth the district's disciplinary notice and hearing procedures. New Jersey and West Virginia both have code sections that require procedural due process for a student accused of assaulting a school employee before a suspension can take place.[30]

State statutes in Michigan, Montana, New Mexico, North Carolina, North Dakota, and Vermont expect school boards to adopt regulations governing the suspension and expulsion of students, but there is no oversight mechanism provided to ensure that students are provided due process or district compliance.

The length of a short-term suspension varies among the states. While a majority have adopted the Supreme Court's definition of ten days, a few states have chosen a lesser time period. For example, Maryland and New York have a five-day limit, Idaho has a five-day limit that can be extended to seven days under certain circumstances, and Texas has a six-day limit. While the education codes of Arizona, Georgia, North Carolina, and North Dakota make no mention of pre-suspension due process, the length of a suspension, in each state, is limited to ten days.

A number of states address the use of disciplinary alternatives to external suspension. California's statutes state that "suspension shall be imposed only when other means of correction fail to bring about proper conduct." Nevertheless, students may be suspended for certain first offenses if the school administrator deems it necessary or if "the pupil's presence causes a danger to persons or property or threatens to disrupt the instructional process."[31] This section was further limited by section 48915, which states that an administrator "*shall* recommend a pupil's expulsion" if the pupil has caused "serious physical injury to another person, except in self-defense," possesses a weapon on school grounds or at school activities, sells drugs on campus, "except for the first offense of the sale of not more than one avoirdupois ounce of marijuana, other than concentrated cannabis," and extortion or robbery. However, an administrator, in the written report, may also recommend that, due to the particular circumstance

Table 4.1
Statutory or Regulatory Response
to Short-Term Suspension Due Process

States[1]

	AL	AK	AZ	AR	CA	CO	CT	DE	FL	GA	HI	ID	IL	IN	KA	KY	LA	MA	ME	MD
1. State has statute giving Goss minimum procedures	X	X		X		X				X			X		X	X	X	X	X	X
2. State had adm. regs. giving Goss minimum procedures	X		X							X							X			
3. State has statute re-requiring districts to develop policies giving Goss minimum procedures					X															
4. State has adm. regs. requiring districts to develop policies giving Goss minimum procedures						X														
5. State has statute giving post-suspension procedures												X								
6. State has no statute mentioning suspension or expulsion						X														

[1]A list of the states with the zip code abbreviation herein used is given below.

Alabama	AL	Hawaii	HI	Massachusetts	MA
Alaska	AK	Idaho	ID	Michigan	MI
Arizona	AZ	Illinois	IL	Minnesota	MN
Arkansas	AR	Indiana	IN	Mississippi	MS
California	CA	Iowa	IA	Missouri	MO
Colorado	CO	Kansas	KA	Montana	MT
Connecticut	CT	Kentucky	KY	Nebraska	NE
Delaware	DE	Louisiana	LA	Nevada	NV
Florida	FL	Maine	ME	New Hampshire	NH
Georgia	GA	Maryland	MD	New Jersey	NJ

MA	MI	MN	MS	MO	MT	NE	NV	NH	NJ	NM	NY	NC	ND	OH	OK	OR	PA	RI	SC	SD	TN	TX	UT	VT	VA	WA	WV	WI	WY
x		x		x	x	x				x			x		x		x	x	x					x	x		x	x	
																	x	x	x	x						x	x		
																						x							

New Mexico	NM	South Dakota	SD
New York	NY	Tennessee	TN
North Carolina	NC	Texas	TX
North Dakota	ND	Utah	UT
Ohio	OH	Vermont	VT
Oklahoma	OK	Virginia	VA
Oregon	OR	Washington	WA
Pennsylvania	PA	West Virginia	WV
Rhode Island	RI	Wisconsin	WI
South Carolina	SC	Wyoming	WY

of the case, expulsion is inappropriate.[32] The state of Georgia provides special funding for in-school suspension. It also requires that parents be informed as to the length of time a student will spend in that alternative program. Arkansas, Indiana, Maryland, Pennsylvania, South Carolina, and Tennessee all permit in-school suspension, but students must receive due process before being placed in the program.[33] As of 1991–92, Mississippi school boards must establish alternative schools for students facing long-term suspensions or expulsion. Minnesota includes the use of alternative disciplinary procedures in its student discipline act. Texas's administrative regulations list a number of disciplinary alternatives including the creation of school-community guidance centers, and its disciplinary statute requires a principal to conduct an investigation before assigning a student to an alternative education program. New York and South Carolina require procedural due process before students receive an involuntary lateral transfer.

Although only the procedural due process requirements in disciplinary situations that might result in short-term suspensions are defined in *Goss*, the Court mentioned that more formal procedures are probably required when either long-term suspension or expulsion is being considered. The education codes and administrative regulations revealed that school districts must provide more formal due process to students facing long-term suspension and/or expulsion in thirty-seven states. The additional states are Arizona, Georgia, Illinois, and Texas. In Mississippi, hearings are held only if requested by the parents or guardians.

The procedures to be followed before a student is removed from school for an extended period are extensive in most of the states. Wisconsin, for example, requires that a formal hearing must be held; the student and parent/guardian must receive written notice of the hearing a minimum of five days before it is to be held. The notice must specify the charges, the time, and the place of the hearing and state the fact that the hearing may result in the pupil's expulsion; the student has a right to counsel and the school board must keep written minutes of the hearing.[34] In Pennsylvania, during the formal hearing, the student has the right to be represented by counsel, the right to a list of the witnesses and copies of their statements and affidavits, the right to request the presence of any witnesses, the right to cross-examine, and the right to testify and present his/her own witnesses.[35] In addition, a record must be kept of the hearing, and the student is entitled, and his/her expense, to a copy of the transcript.[36] California's and Connecticut's codes provide similar procedural requirements.

State-level policies have limited local decision-making authority, as Nolte predicted it would, and in some states there was opposition, initially, to the change. But, as Strope documented in his study of the impact of *Goss* in Nebraska, educators learned to live with it.[37] When, in 1978, a

Nebraska state senator introduced legislation to repeal the existing statute, both the Nebraska State School Boards Association and the Nebraska Council of School Administrators opposed the action. Having lived with the statute for three years, local educators felt it protected both students' rights and their decision-making authority.[38]

LITIGATION AFTER *GOSS* AND ITS
IMPACT ON OTHER EDUCATIONAL DECISIONS

Following *Goss,* suits were pressed to extend the concept of due process to other routine school decisions just as Kola predicted in a number of the areas listed by Weckstein. The results have been mixed. A month after *Goss* was decided, the Supreme Court, in *Wood v. Strickland,* held that school board members can, under certain circumstances, be sued for damages if they violate a student's constitutional rights.[39] Moreover, ignorance of the law is not a defense: "a school board member who has voluntarily undertaken the task of supervising the operation of the school and the activities of the students, must be held to a standard of conduct based not only on permissible intentions, but also on knowledge of the basic, unquestioned constitutional rights of his charges."[40]

The question of whether or not due process was required before a student could be dismissed for academic reasons was also answered by the Supreme Court. In its *Board of Curators of the University of Missouri et al. v. Charlotte Horowitz* decision, the Court stated that there is a "significant difference between the failure of a student to meet academic standards and the violation by a student of valid rules of conduct.[41] This difference calls for far less stringent procedural requirements in the case of an academic dismissal."[42] The Court went on to say that "the determination whether to dismiss a student for academic reasons requires an expert evaluation of cumulative information and is not readily adapted to the procedural tools of judicial or administrative decisionmaking."[43] Historically, the court system has refused to reverse an academic decision unless there was proof that it was arbitrary or capricious, and the Supreme Court, in this instance, continued to decline to "second-guess" the "judgment of educators and thereby formalize the academic dismissal process by requiring a hearing."[44]

The Supreme Court was twice asked if due process is required before a student is subjected to corporal punishment. In *Baker v. Owen,* a federal district court ruled that while school people have the right to administer reasonable corporal punishment they "must accord to a student minimal procedural due process in the course of inflicting such punishment."[45] This decision, appealed to the Supreme Court in 1975, was affirmed without comment. In its 1977 *Ingraham v. Wright* decision, however, the Court concluded that the Fourteenth Amendment's due process clause "does not require notice and a hearing prior to the imposition of corporal punishment in the public schools, as that practice is authorized and limited by the common law."[46]

Although the Supreme Court addressed the due process issue directly in the *Ingraham* decision, lower courts continue to address the same issue. In the vast majority of cases the courts have continued to reject the need for due process before administering corporal punishment unless state or local regulations require it. In *Smith v. West Virginia State Board of Education*, though, the Supreme Court of Appeals of West Virginia ruled that minimal due process procedures should be utilized.[47] While acknowledging *Ingraham*, the court relied on *Goss* and two West Virginia cases, *North v. Board of Regents* and *Waite v. Civil Service Commission*, in making its decision.[48] Moreover, the court issued a writ of mandamus directing the State Board of Education to "promulgate corporal punishment regulations" not inconsistent with the standards set out in its decision.[49]

State and lower federal courts have been asked to expand procedural due process requirements in numerous short-/long-term suspension and expulsion cases, but they have declined to do so. "Unusual situations" claims have also been unsuccessful. When the courts have reversed a school board or administrator's ruling, it has been because of procedural errors in the decision-making process. In *Quier et al. v. Quakertown Community School District*, for example, the court ruled that the school board could not "impose a more severe punishment than the penalty determined by a committee of the board which had been given the authority to determine whether a student should be suspended or expelled."[50]

The question of whether or not students are entitled to "*Miranda* warnings" before making a statement has been answered negatively by the courts. Four months after *Goss*, in a decision that required a rehearing because of procedural errors, a Pennsylvania court rejected all the *Miranda* arguments.[51] The same response was given in cases heard by state and federal courts in Alabama, California, Florida, Maine, Michigan, and New York.[52]

The right of a student or a student's counsel to cross-examine witnesses before a student is suspended or expelled is another issue the courts have been asked to address, and their responses have been mixed. For example, the Sixth Circuit Court of Appeals in *Newsome v. Batavia Local School District*, an expulsion case, concluded that Newsome was "not denied due process by not being permitted to cross-examine or to know the names of his student accusers" or by "not being permitted to cross-examine the school principal and superintendent."[53] Again, in *Paredes by*

Koppenhoefer v. Curtis, a ten-day suspension, the same court cited its *Newsome* decision and ruled "in this less serious suspension case the accused similarly does not have that right."[54] Taking the opposite position, however, were the supreme courts of Mississippi and California. In *Warren County Board of Education v. Wilkinson,* the Mississippi court ruled that the "failure of the Board of Education to have available . . . [the] accusing teachers for examination as requested was a denial of procedural due process to the child."[55] And in *John A. v. San Bernardino City Unified School District,* California's court ruled that while it is legally acceptable, in some situations, for school boards to rely upon administrative statements and reports when revealing the names of student witnesses and requiring their testimony could "subject them to a substantial risk of retaliation," in the instant case that was not true.[56] The witnesses were known and "there was no showing that they were unwilling to testify or that by testifying they would subject themselves to a substantial risk of harm."[57]

Attempts to require due process before suspending a student from an athletic team or other extracurricular activities have consistently met with failure. In *Palmer by Palmer v. Merluzzi,* the court stated that the student had no property or liberty interest in participating in the school's football program.[58] And in *Boster v. Philpot* the court said "a student has no constitutionally protected property interest in *participating* in extracurricular activities."[59] Because there is no property or liberty interest, due process is not required.

School officials may move or transfer students from their "home" school for programmatic, public policy, or disciplinary reasons. The question of whether or not due process is required before a disciplinary transfer (also referred to as an involuntary lateral transfer) can be made has been the subject of a few court cases. Federal courts in Pennsylvania addressed this issue in *Everett v. Marcase* and *Jordan v. School District of City of Erie, Pennsylvania.*[60] In the first instance, the court concluded "that such transfers involve protected property interest of the pupils and are of sufficient significance as to warrant the shelter of due process protection."[61] In the second instance, the court stated that when students are facing the possibility of being transferred from their regularly assigned school to another school for disciplinary reasons they are entitled to due process protection. A Florida state court heard the same question and ruled that the state's education code required due process before disciplinary transfer could be made—that such an action wasfunctionally equivalent to a suspension.[62]

The due process issue was also raised when an Alabama school district transferred students for public policy reasons. School officials, for desegregation purposes, transferred a group of students from a graded to an ungraded school. Standardized reading and math tests were used to determine student placement. Parents who disagreed with their children's placement asserted that the children had been denied due process. The court disagreed. The transfer had not been disciplinary in nature, and the school to which the children were assigned had a superior rating.[63]

In-school suspensions and "time-out" spaces, alternatives to out-of-school suspensions, have been the subject of another group of cases. The courts, when addressing this issue, looked at the length of a student's removal from the regular classroom, the deprivation involved, and the quality of the educational alternative. In addition, the courts looked to see if in-school suspension was being used to evade complying with *Goss*. In *Cole v. Newton Special Municipal Separate School District*, a federal court ruled that plaintiff Walsh's six-day stay in a detention room, which isolated her from her classmates and excluded her from regular classes, "could well constitute as much of a deprivation of education as an at-home suspension."[64] The court went on to say, "this is not to say that any in-school detention would necessarily be equivalent to a suspension; it would depend on the extent to which the student was deprived of instruction or the opportunity to learn."[65] In this case, however, the court denied the defendant school district's motion on the procedural due process and equal protection claims of the plaintiff Walsh. In *Fenton v. Stear,* the plaintiff received a three-day in-school suspension that the court stated did not violate his constitutional rights because he had received the appropriate due process.[66] Moreover, he was not deprived of any in-school education. In *Dickens by Dickens v. Johnson County Board of Education,* however, the court found the need for due process unnecessary.[67] The plaintiff had been placed in a "time-out box" within the classroom (which permitted him to continue to participate in the educational process) because he had repeatedly disrupted the learning environment, and the issue, according to the court, was whether "isolating a student within the classroom amounts to 'a total exclusion from the educational process for more than a trivial period', or whether it amounts to no more than a *de minimis* interference." of the plaintiff's property and liberty interests.[68] The court ruled the latter. While "prolonged, uninterrupted confinement to a 'timeout' area might give rise to a constitutional claim, plaintiff's punishment was not unduly harsh; was not grossly disproportionate to his offense; and was rationally related to a legitimate purpose."[69] Other courts, addressing the use of the same discipline tool, have made similar rulings.

Students have also challenged the disciplinary sentences imposed asserting that their offenses did not require such harsh punishments. Although the courts, in some instances, have been sympathetic to a student's plight, they have not reversed the decisions of the defendant school officials. *Clinton Municipal School District v. Byrd* is such a case.[70] Two of a number of students were discovered painting a three foot high "1" on a school wall (part of a "We're No. 1" message) and, following a full school board hearing, were suspended for the remainder of the school year. While the plaintiffs agreed that some punishment was appropriate, they argued that the length of the suspension was "impermissibly severe in that it is a punishment substantially disproportionate to the 'crime'"— that it violated the plaintiffs' substantive due process rights.[71] The court disagreed. While the court found the punishment to be harsh, "there are many punishments which (perhaps in combination) seem to us more appropriate than that which the school board has determined," the decision of the board violated "no rule of law which has been called to our attention, nor any right secured to these girls by any such rule."[72] The court did note, however, that while "a school rule may be worded in mandatory language [it] does not deprive school boards and their subordinates of the authority to administer the rule with flexibility and leniency."[73] A board may choose otherwise but "in doing so . . . it may not hide behind the notion that the law prohibits leniency for there is no such law."[74] In another case, *Lamb v. Panhandle Community Unit School District No. 2,* a student was suspended for the last three days of school.[75] He missed his final exams, failed three classes, and was unable to graduate. He claimed that because of the results, the disciplinary sentence was equivalent to an expulsion and, therefore, additional due process was required. The court disagreed. The court cited another case that had dealt with the same issue and said, "the *Keough* court held that more formal procedures than a discussion between the student and principal were not required, merely because the original ten-day suspension occurred during final exams and thus had a long-term effect."[76] This was also true in this instance—"despite the long-term effects of the principal's action, it did not amount to an expulsion."[77]

Although the courts have, for the most part, refrained from reversing academic decisions made by educators, there have been a few exceptions to that policy. The *Debra P. v. Turlington* case, first tried in a Florida federal district court in 1979, reviewed by the Fifth Circuit in 1981, and tried again by the district court in 1983, is one such example.[78] In 1978, the Florida legislature enacted legislation requiring public school students to pass a functional literacy exam in order to receive a high school diploma. Shortly thereafter, a class-action suit was filed challenging the constitutionality of the test requirement, claiming that it violated both the equal protection and due process clauses of the Constitution. After reviewing the evidence, the court was of the opinion that "the inadequacy of the notice provided prior to the invocation of the diploma sanction, the objectives, and the test is a violation of the due process clause."[79] In making its ruling the court relied upon expert testimony that indicated that "four to six years should intervene between the announcement of the objectives and the implementation of the diploma sanction."[80] This being the case, the court decided "the implementation schedule in effect relative to the functional literacy testing program with the diploma sanction is fundamentally unfair" and enjoined the use of the test as a diploma requirement until the 1982–83 academic year.[81] In response to a question about whether or not the test being utilized had content validity, however, the court found that its validity was "adequate." Both parties appealed the decision to the Fifth Circuit Court of Appeals. The appeals court upheld the trial court's finding that the test implementation timetable violated due process. But, it went on to say, "We believe that the state administered a test that was, at least on the record before us, fundamentally unfair in that it *may* have covered matters not taught in the schools of the state."[82] Because "an important component of content validity is curricular validity" and the record "is simply insufficient in proof that the test administered measures what was actually taught in the school of Florida," the content validity holding was reversed.[83] The appeals court decided that "fundamental fairness requires that the state be put to test on the issue of whether the students were tested on material they were or were not taught" and remanded the case back to the district court to decide the question.[84] When the district court reheard the case it found, after listening to all the expert testimony presented, that the functional literacy examination did have curricular validity and ruled that the injunction should not be extended.

Students have claimed that their due process rights were violated when they lost academic credit or their grades were reduced because of misconduct or truancy. In cases such as *Slocum v. Holton Board of Education, Knight v. Board of Education of Tri-Point Community School District No. 6J,* and *Campbell v. Board of Education of New Milford,* no due process violations were determined, and the decisions of the school authorities were upheld.[85] In *Katzman v. Cumberland Valley School District,* however, the appellant court affirmed the trial court's decision that the school board had illegally applied its discretionary powers and that the grade reduction was improper.[86]

The right of homeless children to attend school has also raised due process questions. In both *White by White v. Linkinoggor* and *Harrison v. Sobol,* the courts found that the students' exclusion from school were violations of their due process rights.[87]

The newest area in which the due process question has arisen, in the K-12 educational arena, concerns excluding students who refused to submit urine samples for drug testing. *Odenheim v. Carlstadt-East Rutherford Regional School District* addressed this issue.[87] The school district's new student physical examination policy required a drug-screening urinalysis designed to detect the presence of controlled dangerous substances (which were defined in the district's policy). Failure to submit to the exam or to provide an incomplete exam carried a sanction of exclusion from class. Moreover, "the parent or legal guardian of the pupil will be advised of a penalty which may be imposed upon the parent or legal guardian pursuant to N.J.S.A. 18A:40-9 when such parent or legal guardian fails, within a reasonable time, to remedy the cause for exclusion."[89] The plaintiffs charged that said policy violated a student's right to be free of unreasonable search and seizure, due process, and a legitimate expectation of privacy and personal security, all constitutional safeguards. The court rejected the school district's claim that the "exclusion of students pursuant to Policy No. 5141.3 is distinguishable from expulsion or suspension of student under N.J.S.A. 18A:37-2(j) as the former is for medical reasons, while the latter is purely disciplinary."[90] Finding the attempted distinction unacceptable, the court stated that the policy "is an attempt to control student discipline under the guise of a medical procedure, thereby circumventing strict due process requirements."[91] Judgment was entered on behalf of the plaintiffs.

Student due process rights have had the greatest expansion in the area of special education. Sue Simon, in a 1984 article, wrote that P.L.94-142 and Section 504 of the Rehabilitation Act of 1973 have been interpreted by the Fifth and Sixth Circuit Courts as guaranteeing "handicapped students more extensive procedural safeguards than are ordinarily accorded to nonhandicapped students facing disciplinary proceedings.[92] This same interpretation has been accepted by other federal and state courts since that article was written. There was one major issue that caused considerable controversy, and the Supreme Court addressed it in 1988. In *Honig v. Doe,* the Court was asked if the Education of the Handicapped Act's "stay-put" provision prohibits a school district from suspending a student pending the completion of any review proceedings.[93] By the time the Court made its decision the case was moot as to respondent Doe but was justiciable to the second respondent, Smith. Both respondents "were emotionally disturbed students [who] were suspended indefinitely for violent and disruptive conduct related to their disabilities, pending the completion of expulsion proceedings by the San Francisco Unified School District."[94] The Court ruled that EHA's language is unequivocal, that there is not a "'dangerousness' exception to the stay-put provision."[95] The Court concluded "that Congress very much meant to strip schools of the *unilateral* authority they had traditionally employed to exclude disabled students, particularly emotionally disturbed students, from school."[96] Such a conclusion does not leave educators "hamstrung," the Court believed, because school personnel may use their "normal procedures for dealing with children who are endangering themselves or others." Disciplinary alternatives such as the "use of study carrels, timeouts, detention, or the restriction of privileges" are all acceptable.[97] And "where a student poses an immediate threat to the safety of others, officials may temporarily suspend him or her for up to 10 school days."[98] A suspension in excess of that period, however, would constitute a "change in placement."[99] The Court also said that if "the parents of a truly dangerous child adamantly refuse to permit any change in placement, the 10-day respite gives school officials an opportunity to invoke the aid of the courts."[100]

The use of legally acceptable alternatives to suspension procedures that Hazard believed schools might search for, such as those mentioned by the Supreme Court, has increased in schools across the nation since *Goss* was decided. The following section reviews the literature on these methods, both the rhetoric and the reality.

DISCIPLINARY ALTERNATIVES TO SUSPENSION

Some members of the school community have, for years, used the penalty of suspension or expulsion with great infrequency. Instead of totally separating a student from the educational experience, they have employed a variety of disciplinary alternatives to modify unacceptable behavior. Others, however, found exclusionary penalties a quick and easy way to rid themselves of problematic students, at least temporarily. There was a movement afoot, however, to reassess the usefulness of off-campus suspensions. *Goss,* and then *Wood,* provided the needed incentive to reevaluate past practices and explore, more fully, other methods for dealing with disruptive behavior. The National Institute of Education, for example, held a conference entitled "In-School Alternative to Suspension" in 1978 to examine the issue, and a group of papers were presented that discussed reactions to the use of suspension and various in-school alternatives. Hayes Mizell, for example, noted that suspending students who had committed attendance offenses was "an irrational and ineffective disciplinary response" that compounded the problems of unexcused absences from class or school.[101] Suspension was not the "most effective or productive response to a variety of nonviolent, nonovertly disruptive offenses" either.[102] Students who were suspended were more apt to get into trouble in the community, especially if they were "unsupervised and uninvolved in constructive activity."[103] And school people had realized that suspended students do not generate funds because they are not counted in the average daily attendance (in states where state aid is based on ADA).

Reviews of the various types of disciplinary alternatives have been done by a number of researchers. After analyzing a number of studies, Norma Radin identified eight that are being used most often: timeout, in-school suspension, Saturday school, alternative schools, behavioral contracting, use of peers, use of parents, and social/cognitive skills training.[104]

Timeout procedures, which were mentioned by the Supreme Court, are used when disruptive students are removed from the classroom for a very short period to permit them to regain their self-control. Such students may sit in a chair in the central office, in an isolated portion of the library, or in a separate room. They are usually permitted to return to the classroom after they have had a conversation about their behavior with a school official.

In-school suspensions are used when a student's behavior is such that he/she is being removed from the classroom for a longer period of time. These suspensions have a simple and an elaborate form. Schools using the simple form send students to a room with their classroom assignments where they spend the day(s) working on those materials under the supervision of a professional or para-professional employee. They have no contact with the general school population; they eat lunch in the room and conversation is limited to discussions with the supervisor concerning academic assignments. When the more elaborate form is used, students may be provided with guidance materials to help them to analyze their own behavior. In addition to academic and behavior modification assignments, they also receive counseling.

Saturday schools have been instituted by some districts for students with truancy records or unexcused absence. Some instruction is usually provided during these sessions.

Alternative or continuation schools have been developed by a number of districts because research has shown that "placing disruptive secondary school pupils in a different educational context can lead to improved behavior, more positive attitudes toward school and enhanced learning."[105] Staffed by a faculty that usually has chosen to teach in this alternative environment, classroom structure and instruction are more individualized and flexible. While a majority of these schools' populations are there because of disciplinary problems, some members choose to attend because they have found the more traditional educational setting to be an alienating experience.

Rather than suspending a student, in or out of school, some school administrators have used behavior contracts as a means to correct misbehavior. A written contract is drawn up between the student and teacher (or administrator) defining the behavior problem(s); the student and teacher both state what they will do to help to improve the situation, and an agreed upon penalty is determined if the contract is not fulfilled.

The use of student peers to help control recalcitrant students is also being used in a number of districts. Elementary as well as secondary school administrators have created student disciplinary committees to assist in dealing with problems and finding solutions.

Parents, obviously, play an important role in disciplinary situations. School districts have involved parents in a variety of ways. Radin described one district that established a parent disciplinary committee, similar to the student committee described above, to handle behavior problems. Behavior modification programs that involve parental support and daily report cards sent home to parents have been used by some others. In California, a few districts have invited parents to observe their children in the classroom setting.

The final procedure is social/cognitive skills training used to "teach aggressive children self-management and interpersonal problem-solving skills." [106] This procedure, to be most effective, has to be used in conjunction with other strategies employed by a school district. It also involves the use of skilled social workers.

The literature review on disciplinary alternatives to suspension also reveals articles written by school personnel describing programs being operated in their school districts. The *National Association of Secondary School Principals Bulletin* is a primary source of these materials. School faculty members at a California junior high school, for example, discussed the kind of personnel needed to run a successful on-campus program, the contract students need to sign, the test materials used to determine the students' academic abilities and interests, and the rules and regulations that govern the students assigned to the suspension room. [107] And, in Pennsylvania, an assistant principal described a Saturday plan that his small district instituted for students in grades 4 through 12. [108] Discussed in his article are the program costs, the staffing requirements, the operational guidelines, the students who must attend, and parental and community response.

Although the educators in the above two examples believe their programs have had a positive impact, not all alternative disciplinary programs have been successful. While the rhetoric has been promising, the reality is quite a different story, according to two researchers who studied in-school suspension programs for the North Carolina Governor's Crime Commission. [109] Ten programs nominated by state education and juvenile justice officials were the subject of the study. After analyzing the data, which included written documents, interviews, and site visits, the researchers concluded that there was very little variation in the majority of the programs. "All were essentially punitive" in nature. They all had academic components, but in the students' view the academic work appeared to be part of the punishment. The lessons supplied by the classroom teachers "were usually insufficient to fill the offender's day," the supervising teachers "often reported they were unable to assist students with their lessons given the teachers' limited subject areas and the breadth of the students' coursework," and the lessons "presumed the students had received and understood instruction in the mechanics of completing the lessons."[110] The researchers did note, however, that some of the ISS rooms "emphasized academics more than others by having auxiliary materials, learning centers, and more academically oriented milieu."[111] Only one school program's included counseling and behavioral programming. More importantly, however, that school "had other distinguishing features. It had implemented a total school discipline program based on a philosophy of positive behavioral expectations."[112] A number of disciplinary alternatives were used by the school, and it was the only one "that had a system for assessing the effects of the program."[113] Therefore, while in-school suspension may be more desirable than out-of-school suspension, it is a limited innovation.

The above study was completed in 1983, eight years after *Goss* was decided. It illustrates the use of legally acceptable alternatives to suspension that Hazard suggested has clearly occurred in various parts of the country. He also suggested that pre- and in-service training concerning students' constitutional rights might be provided to help bring about change. Did that also happen? It is now sixteen years later. Did procedural due process become a mere formality, as Levine predicted it might, or has it had an impact on the disciplinary process? Buss suggested four possible responses by the educational community: (1) *Goss* would change nothing either because of ignorance or lawlessness; (2) school leaders would give "lip service" to the procedure, but it would be "business as usual;" (3) administrators would be intimidated by *Goss* and forsake their disciplinary responsibilities, and (4) the procedural guidelines given by the Court would enhance and strengthen administrative authority, protect students' rights and create a climate of fair and open-minded treatment. Have any of these possibilities become reality? Has the passage of time, itself, had an impact on people's perceptions concerning a student's right to procedural due process? Are students suspended for a first offense, and, if so, what offenses prompt immediate exclusion? Are other attempts to modify socially unacceptable behavior used for some offenses, and are they punitive, academic, or therapeutic in nature? Do administrators feel pressured to suspend students in order to maintain the support of their faculty and staff? What has been the impact on administrative discretionary authority? And finally, do administrators feel that due process impedes the disciplinary process and seriously erodes their discretionary authority? The following section of this chapter addresses these questions.

PRESENT DAY DUE PROCESS AND
ALTERNATIVE DISCIPLINARY PRACTICES

To answer the above questions, I conducted a study of disciplinary practices and procedures in four southern California public school districts. All the districts have heterogeneous populations and serve approximately 120,000 students. All have written disciplinary policies that comply with California's education code.[114] Included in these policies are the grounds for suspension and expulsion, the length and number of suspensions permissible in an academic year, the required use of other means of correction before suspending or expelling for certain offenses, the procedural due process to be provided before a student is suspended or expelled, and the procedures for appealing an expulsion to a county board of education.

The data sources included on-site visits and interviews with principals and vice principals serving elementary, middle, and high schools, central office personnel, written documents, and first-hand knowledge of in-service training activities that were presented shortly after *Goss* was decided. Twenty-four people were interviewed. Twenty were site administrators, twelve at the elementary level, four at the middle/junior, and four at the high school level. The other four interviewees were district office personnel who supervise child welfare and attendance—administrators whose responsibilities include such activities as compiling statistical data on suspensions and expulsions; arranging and overseeing expulsion hearings; meeting with students who are facing expulsion, and their parents, to inform them of their procedural rights and to provide information about the hearing process; chairing disciplinary hearing committees; providing and/or arranging in-service training to site personnel; and overseeing district-wide alternative educational programs for students with disciplinary problems.

The sample selection was not random. Although the districts included in the study were chosen because they serve heterogeneous populations, the participants were selected by the districts themselves. When discussing the project with central office personnel, the statement was made that this study is a "reality check" on what is actually happening on elementary, middle, and high school campuses today. Therefore, the administrators chosen to participate should be serving at these three levels and should have disciplinary responsibilities. In addition, if any site administrators dealing directly with discipline had pre-*Goss* experience, they were to be included in the sample. As a result, twenty-five percent of the sample are people who were administrators before 1975. The other seventy-five percent of the site administrators have administrative tenure ranging from one to fifteen years. In addition to their administrative credentials, three also have counseling credentials and/or counseling experience. Eight of the participants are female, twelve are male, six are black, thirteen are white, one is Hispanic, and all serve integrated student populations. The socioeconomic status of the student bodies ranges from abject poverty to extreme wealth, but none of the schools are made up of a single socioeconomic class. Socioeconomic diversity has been achieved in a variety of ways—revised attendance boundaries, busing, magnet programs, and choice. All of the schools are having to help their student bodies deal with some level of violence, either on or off campus. Some of the sites have a high rate of transiency. All of the high schools have dress-code policies prohibiting the wearing of gang colors or clothing that can be identified with gangs.[115] Because of the population explosion, some sites are made up entirely of portable classrooms, some have brand new buildings, and others have well-established campuses.

History and current practices provide the answer to the question of whether or not in-service training concerning students' constitutional due process rights. Shortly after *Goss* was decided, at the request of the county superintendents, the offices of the County Counsel provided in-service training for interested school personnel explaining the implications of the decision and answering questions about the process and the procedures. Since that time the County Counsels and the University of California, Riverside, education faculty have provided additional assistance to districts requesting it. Districts also sponsor periodic training sessions for administrators and faculty that review policies, procedures, and changes in state law.

Biographical data revealed that time itself has had a significant impact on administrators' perceptions of student due process. Of the more than 175 school-site administrators with the authority to suspend for five days or recommend expulsion, only five held administrative positions before 1975. All those who have received administrative credentials post-*Goss* have studied the decision in a school law class and, as was true in the Indiana study, recognized that *Goss* is a Supreme Court decision. While a number no longer remember what it says, they are fully knowledgeable about both the statutes and their district's disciplinary policies.[116] Today, procedural due process is the norm for the principals, vice-principals, and deans serving in these four districts. There was no distinguishable difference in the way pre- and post-*Goss* administrators discussed how they went about suspending students.

When asked if students are suspended for a first offense the answer was a qualified "yes." California's statutes and district policies list twelve groups of offenses for which students can be suspended or expelled. Administrators must suspend students found to be guilty of the first five: possessing a weapon on campus, fighting and causing bodily injury, possessing or selling drugs or alcohol, and robbery/extortion. They must also suspend students found guilty of committing arson on school premises. Unless there are extenuating circumstances, a written recommendation for extended suspension/expulsion will be made to the superintendent's office. Once such a recommendation goes forward, the burden of responsibility shifts to central office personnel who provide further and more formal procedural protection.

Depending upon the circumstances, school officials are also required to call for police assistance. This is always done when a student possesses a gun or when drugs are involved. The latter situation occurred while this researcher was on a school campus. A school administrator learned, through the grapevine, that a student was believed to have a controlled substance on his person. The student was summoned to the office, told the reason why he was there, asked to empty his pockets, and then told that a further check would be made. One pocket was searched and eight bags of marijuana were found. The student then reached into another pocket and said, "Here are four more." The student acknowledged his possession of the drug but did not explain why he had them. The police were called to the campus, the student was arrested, the twelve bags were removed to be tested to determine legally the contents, and the student was transported to the police station for booking. The administrator called and informed the student's parents of the incident and asked that they come to the school with their child after he was released to their custody. About two hours later the student and one of his parents met with the administrator. During that meeting the administrator told the parent what had happened, reviewed the law, and informed the student that he would be suspended for five days. Because of the seriousness of the offense the administrator also stated that an expulsion recommendation would be forwarded to the central office. The student acknowledged that he had done wrong and that the administrator had been fair in dealing with the situation. The parent, who was very angry with the son, agreed and thanked the administrator.

Administrators may choose to suspend or use alternative methods of correction when students commit the other seven groups: causing or damaging school or private property, attempting to or stealing school or private property, smoking on campus, committing an obscene act or engaging in habitual profanity or vulgarity, selling drug paraphernalia, disrupting school activities or willful defiance, and knowingly receiving stolen school or private property. When alternative efforts fail to modify behavior, then a student will be suspended. Such was the case at an elementary school site. The day the site was visited a student was sitting in a small room adjacent to the main office waiting for his parents to take him home. The principal stated that he has a "mouth" problem and was being suspended for cursing a teacher. A number of willful defiance incidents had occurred prior to this event, student and parental conferences had been held, and the student had been moved to another classroom to get special assistance because of a learning problem. On that day he had "mouthed off" at the teacher and had been removed from the classroom to cool off. When he was given a referral notice to take to the principal, he used a number of profanities to tell the teacher what he thought of her. During the meeting with the principal he denied everything, and an investigation was conducted to determine the truth in the matter. Student witnesses confirmed the teachers' charges, and the student was suspended for five days.

The schools in this study do use alternative methods to correct behavior. Whether these alternatives were developed as a direct response to *Goss* is difficult to determine, but a wide variety are in place in every district. Many are punitive in nature but there are also academic and therapeutic alternatives. They also differ, to some degree, by grade level. Most of those used at the elementary level are punitive. The most common are conferences, first with the students and then with parents, time-outs, benching, denial of privileges, detention during recess, lunch recess, or after school. At two sites, after school detention cannot be used because at least half of the student population is bussed to those schools. Elementary schools lack the space or the staff available to do a traditional in-school suspension. Moreover, a number of the elementary administrators do not believe in that disciplinary alternative. Said one principal, who rarely uses suspension, "If the misdeed is severe enough that the child does not belong in class, he or she does not belong in school." Teachers may, however, send a student to another teachers' room to work on assignments, usually in the back of the room, for the remainder of the day. In one school, a student disciplinary committee also works with students. Student study teams are available and teachers will request that a team meeting be held to review a student's record and provide assistance. Referrals to a school administrator usually occur only after other efforts have proved unsuccessful. As one administrator said, "I am the 'big gun' and it is the 1 or 2 percent who cannot be brought under control that make the trip to my office." Only one school has a certified counselor, and she is serving in an administrative capacity. Two principals use behavior contracts with students, if the parents are cooperative, and have found them to be effective. At one site the principal and vice-principal both do role playing and simulations with students. That principal also has the misbehaving student call the parent(s) and tell them of his/her misdeed(s). Occasionally, administrators will assign an elementary student to Saturday school in lieu of suspension. Due to budget constraints academic alternatives are virtually nonexistent. On a more positive note, however, some school sites do have programs and activities to encourage and acknowledge positive behavior. Regular attendance, academic achievement, good deeds, etc. are given recognition at assemblies and "spirit" days. Local businesses have been solicited to provide rewards for students, and the P.T.A. also makes contributions. One site has a number of extracurricular activities to keep students busy both during the lunch hour and after school.

Middle and junior high school administrators and faculty, in addition to using many of the above punitive alternatives, also utilize in-school suspension—supervision provided by a campus aide. At one campus the principal has asked some parents to come and spend the day at school with their children. In every case the parent has never had to come back. The students are so embarrassed that they work very diligently to change their behavior. Also, at this site, students who have a difficult time controlling their behavior in the afternoon (they get "antsy") may be put on a modified schedule. Because they are not permitted to attend assemblies, participate in intramural sports and other social activities, however, "they are soon begging to come back to school for the full schedule." At another site, there is an after-school work program during which time student may clean classrooms, the campus, or take rocks off the baseball field. Parents will sometimes ask that their children be assigned to this program rather than be suspended.

The middle schools also provide academic and therapeutic alternatives. All offer opportunity programs, but because of budget constraints only a limited number of students can be served. Independent study programs are also available to some students. One site has a "school within a school" for students who have problems with self-control. In addition to their academic assignments, these students work on developing self-esteem and coping and organizational skills. Another has a group of seventeen teachers who are trained in group counseling. Each teacher meets one day a week, for an eight-week period, with a small number of students with similar problems to help them to resolve their difficulty. A third has the assistance of a private, outside counseling group.

Although middle schools have more alternatives, more students are suspended and referred for expulsion than at the elementary level. Statistical data from the districts show an increase in the number of physical harm and weapons violations. As one middle school administrator said, "Some children have problems adjusting to their new environment and act out, for the first time, at this age level." Parents have also commented, to this person, that their children are behaving differently, that they did not behave this way in elementary school.

Punitive, academic, and therapeutic alternatives to suspension are all employed at the high schools that participated in this study. Full-time counselors are available at all the schools, and, at one site, students who have been cited for willful defiance are automatically referred to the counseling office. Students with academic deficiencies often work with counselors, and one campus has the services of a psychologist to assist in identifying learning deficiencies. Another campus has an after-school homework program for students, which is held in the library. Teachers sign up for different days and provide one-on-one assistance. A peer-counseling program also functions at that site. Another campus has a "school within a school" staffed by six teachers. One hundred twenty "at-risk" students participate in this program. All have contracted to be in the program, and they must maintain a full academic load. In addition, attention is given to building self-esteem, goal setting, learning that it is okay to like and do well in school.

There are fewer detention programs used at the senior high level. Students may be assigned, either by an administrator or a teacher, to after-school detention. Students given this penalty may either sit in a supervised classroom and do assigned work, or they may clean up the campus. School administrators often assign students to on-campus detention (o.c.d.) when students fail to show up for after-school detention, when they have been suspended from a specific class four times, or in lieu of off-campus suspension. Students normally spend no more than a day or two in o.c.d. At one site, o.c.d. runs forty-five minutes longer than the normal school day. The administrators discovered that some students were deliberately missing their after-school detention assignments and opting for o.c.d. so that they could meet their friends at the end of the day. The time change has discouraged that practice—there has been a dramatic drop in the number of students in o.c.d. State law requires that districts have continuation high schools, and the majority of students on these campuses have either academic or disciplinary problems. There is extensive use made of Saturday schools, the classes populated by students with records of truancies or excess absences.

There are also district-wide programs for students, though there are very few at the elementary level. One district sponsors a Steps for Success program for students on extended suspension, suspended expulsion, or expelled (there are also a few non-suspended students enrolled).[117] Schools may also refer students with poor attendance records to S.A.R.B., the Student Attendance Review Board, which provides considerable assistance. One district has a counseling center, sponsored by a neighboring hospital, to assist students and their families. And two districts can refer students to county-sponsored community schools or an independent study program.

When asked if a teacher's request to have a student suspended from the school campus is usually affirmed, the administrators stated that very few teachers actually make such requests. Teachers have the legal authority to suspend a student from their classroom for the day of the violation and an additional day. Those choosing to do so must provide due process to the student, contact the parents (and meet with them if that is possible), and file a written report for the office. According to two principals, their teachers do not use this very often because they do not like doing paperwork. Only one principal mentioned the need to oversee the process to ensure procedures were being followed. Teachers can refer students to the office, but their written referrals normally do not include a suspension request. One principal stated that if a teacher has a number of defiance and discipline referrals, then the principal will observe the classroom activities to determine the causes of the problems. Then, written assistance programs are provided for the teacher as well as follow-up meetings. About half of the elementary administrators mentioned that such problems are usually the result of a teacher's inconsistent classroom management behavior—students sometimes really do not understand what they have done that was considered wrong behavior—and that they spend time helping teachers remedy the situation.

On other occasions the event prompting the referral may require direct action to be taken. When this occurs at the elementary level some principals tell students why they have been sent to the office and ask them to tell their side of the story. Other principals ask students why they have been sent to the office. If the student is unable to answer that question, then the principal will read the referral note to the student and ask for the story to be told. At the middle and high school level, the student is told the charge(s) and then asked to respond. All of the principals said that the majority of students do not deny the charges and want to talk about what happened. When the student denies the charge, then there is a further investigation. Usually there are witnesses to the rule infraction, many of them students, and they are willing to testify. Ofttimes, students report another student's possession of a weapon or drugs to a teacher or a principal so that action can be taken. At one site, for example, a principal learned through the student grapevine that a third-grade student had brought a gun on campus because he had done a "show and tell" with some friends. At another school, an administrator received a tip that weapons and drugs were present in the trunk of a student's car. The student was called to the office, the administrator informed him why he had been summoned, and asked for permission to search the student's vehicle. Permission was granted and the search disclosed some knives, baseball bats that were being carried for protection, and a controlled substance (the car owner did not have knowledge of the latter, a fact confirmed by other students).

Sometimes denial of the charges will prompt an administrator to withhold action until a meeting with a parent, as well as the student, can take place. On other occasions, when a suspended student continues to deny the charges, a parent may appeal the suspension and a meeting will be held to review the evidence. Such an occurrence immediately preceded the interview of one principal. A student had been caught changing her grades. She was referred to the office and told the charge. She denied it and witnesses to the event were brought in to testify. Although she continued to deny the charge, she was suspended for five days. The parent called and requested a meeting. During that meeting the parent learned the misdeed had been witnessed by a number of people, the student was in academic trouble— failing notices had been sent home that the student had intercepted. After receiving all this information, the parent withdrew the request to appeal the suspension.

In response to the question regarding impact on discretionary authority, the responses were mixed. While they must follow the law set down by the legislature and the policies of their districts, they are free to develop discipline policies tailored to meet the needs of their individual school sites. Nine of the administrators discussed these in some detail. They also acknowledge, however, that sometimes they have to suspend a student even when that might not be the best solution to the problem. Such was the case when an elementary school principal had to suspend a second-grade student who had marijuana in his possession. He had found the drug in his home and brought it to school to show his friends. It was clear, after the principal talked with him, that he did not comprehend the consequences of his act. Nevertheless, he had to be suspended for five days. The parents did understand, however, and were embarrassed and very apologetic.

Does procedural due process impede the disciplinary process? This was another question answered ''no.'' The administrators believe the time spent permits them to get a better understanding of most of the problems and to learn more about the students. Two incidents illustrate this fact. The first occurred at an elementary school. A young man was sent to the principal's office because of belligerent behavior. The principal learned that the student, who had recently transferred into the district, was functionally illiterate and that frustration with his learning disability was the primary cause of his negative behavior. Instead of disciplining the student, the principal arranged for additional academic assistance. The student has made great strides, academically, is returning to school for further help during his off-track vacation period, and is no longer a discipline problem.

The second occurred at a middle school. A young woman with an "attitude" problem finally landed in the vice-principal's office. The vice-principal read the charge on the referral slip and asked the student to tell her story. In the midst of recounting the incident the student broke down and said that she just could not cope any more. Life at home was in shambles, and she was stressed out. The vice-principal decided to take a chance and gave the student a pass, saying, "Any time you feel you are going to blow you use this pass and come and see me. I will let your teachers know you have it and it is okay for you to come." Since then the vice-principal has seen the student in the halls, but she has never used the pass. Nor has she been in any more trouble.

None of these school districts have had to go to court to defend their disciplinary decisions. There have been a number of expulsion decisions appealed to the two counties' boards of education but the majority have been affirmed by the boards. Those decisions that were overturned were the result of failure to adhere to procedure during some point of the process.

CONCLUSIONS

An examination of suspension and expulsion practices sixteen years after *Goss* was handed down reveals that disciplinary practices have not ground to a halt, nor have they been seriously impeded in the four school districts that participated in this study. The administrators do not give "lip service" to the due process procedure; it is a normal and accepted part of the disciplinary process. The overwhelming majority of today's administrators are post-*Goss* appointments and consider due process to be the fair way to function. Moreover, most administrators would prefer not to suspend or expel students; it is a measure used only when all other alternatives have failed to correct negative behavior or to provide a physically safe environment for the student population. The majority of students and parents, while they may not like the suspension sentence, do believe that the procedure is fair, that they are heard, and that their rights are protected. While recognizing that teacher authority needs to be supported, these administrators do not automatically honor a teacher's request that a student be suspended from school. Other alternatives may be used to resolve the problem, and when there are conflicting stories, investigations are made. The authority to suspend a student off campus is vested only to administrators, and they take this responsibility very seriously. State statutes and administrative regulations provide school-site and central office personnel with clear guidelines that protect the rights of both students and school leaders. Administrative discretionary authority is relative and may

may be curtailed more by school board policies than by state policies. In-service training concerning disciplinary procedures and statutes for school-site personnel is provided on a regular basis by the districts. Sixty-six percent of the states have enacted statutory or administrative regulations protecting the procedural rights of students facing short-term suspension, and seventy-four percent have procedural policies governing long-term suspensions and expulsions. The courts have not, in the majority of cases, extended the need for due process into other areas of the educational enterprise. The suspension and expulsion of special education students has been the only major area that the courts have required further procedural protection.

NOTES

1. 87 S.Ct. 1428, 387 U.S. 1 (1967).
2. 463 F.2d, 763 (1972).
3. 468 F.2d, 768, 769.
4. 354 F.Supp. 592 (1973).
5. 95 S.Ct. 729 (1975).
6. *Lopez v. Williams* 372 F.Supp. 1279 (1973), *aff'd sub nom, Goss v. Lopez,* 95 S.Ct. 729 (1975).
7. See note 5.
8. Zimring and Solomon, "*Goss v. Lopez:* The Principle of the Thing," in *In The Interest of Children,* ed. R. Mnookin. One week before the hearing was held, the Columbus school board issued new suspension guidelines that required principals to provide students with notice of the charges and a hearing before a suspension could be enforced.
9. Zimring and Solomon, quoting from an interview with two of the original attorneys for the plaintiffs (474).
10. See *supra* note 5 at 739, 740.
11. *Id.* at 740.
12. *Id.* at 740.
13. Reinhold, "The Supreme Court and the Rights of Pupils: A Challenge Posed to Powers of Schools to Expel or Suspend," *New York Times* 27 Jan. 1975, 16, col. 1.
14. 43 *Fordham Law Review* 1011, 1018 (1975).
15. Townsend, "Due Process Right and High School Suspension After *Goss v. Lopez,*" 36 *Montana Law Review* 333.
16. 420 U.S., 308; 95 S.Ct., 992 (1975).
17. Buss, 1971, "Implications of *Goss v. Lopez,* and *Wood v. Strickland* for Professional Discretion and Liability in School," *Journal of Law Education* 4:567, 574.

18. *Id.* at 574.
19. *Id.*
20. *Id.*
21. *Id.* at 575.
22. Levine, 1975, "Reflections on *Goss v. Lopez*," *Journal of Law Education* 4:579, 582.
23. Kola, 1975, "Hard Choices in School Discipline and the Hardening of the Due Process Mold," *Journal of Law Education* 4:583, 585.
24. Hazard, 1975, "*Goss v. Lopez* and *Wood v. Strickland*: Some Implications for School Practice," *Journal of Law Education* 4:605, 606–9.
25. Weckstein, 1975, "The Supreme Court and the Daily Life of Schools: Implications of *Goss v. Lopez*," *Inequality In Education* 20:47.
26. Nolte, 1975, "The Supreme Court's New Rules for Due Process and How (somehow) Schools Must Make Them Work," *American School Board Journal,* 162:47, 49.
27. Anson., 1975, "The Educator's Response to *Goss* and *Wood*" *Phi Delta Kappan* 57:16.
28. Teitelbaum, 1983, "School Discipline Procedures: Some Empirical Findings and Some Theoretical Questions," *Indiana Law Journal* 58:547, 560–61.
29. A post-suspension hearing was mandatory in Illinois prior to 1972. The hearing became optional when the Code was amended in 1972.
30. If the official believes that the continued presence of the student in school poses a continuing danger, then the student may be suspended immediately and a hearing held as soon as it is practical.
31. *Cal. Educ. Code* sec. 48900.5 (1991).
32. *Cal. Educ. Code* sec. 48915.5 (1991).
33. According to one Pennsylvania official, a few school administrators began using in-school suspension so that they could avoid giving students procedural due process. To prevent this, the state's administrative regulations were amended in 1984, and due process before placing a student in an in-school suspension program was made a requirement.
34. 1979 *Wis. Laws,* chapter 94, sec. 120.13(c).
35. In 1887, in *Commonwealth ex rel. Hill v. McCauley et al.* 3 Pa. C.C. 77, a state court ruled that a hearing or trial in accordance with a lawful form of procedure was required before a student could be dismissed. Shortly thereafter the state legislature enacted a statute requiring that school boards hold a proper hearing before the long-term suspension or expulsion of a student. In 1974, the State Board of Education enacted regulations defining the requirements of a "proper hearing."
36. 22 *Pa. Admin. Code* –12–8 (1984).

37. J. Strope, 1979, "The Impact of the United States Supreme Court on the Education Policies of the States with Particular Emphasis on *Goss v. Lopez* in Nebraska," (Ph.D. diss., University of Nebraska, Lincoln).
38. Nebraska educators had faced three legal challenges concerning suspension/ expulsion decisions following the passage of the new statute, and the courts found for the defendant educators in each instance.
39. 95 S.Ct. 992 (1975)
40. *Id.*
41. 98 S.Ct. 948; 435 U.S. 78; 55 L.Ed. 124 (1987).
42. 98 S.Ct. 948, 953.
43. *Id.*
44. *Id.* at 955.
45. 395 F.Supp. 294, 296, *aff'd mem.* 423 U.S. 907 (1975).
46. 430 U.S. 651.
47. 295 S.E.2d 680 (1982).
48. 233 S.E.2d 411 (1977); 341 S.E.2d 164 (1977).
49. *Supra,* note 43 at 688.
50. 27 *Bucks Co. L. Rep.* 199 (1975).
51. *Minnicks v. McKeesport Area School District,* 74 D. & C.2d 744 (1975).
52. *Adams v. City of Dothan,* 485 So.2d 757 (1986); *In re Corey L.,* 250 Cal. Rptr. 359, 203 C.A.3d 1020, *rev. den.* (1988); *Adams v. School Board of Brevard County,* 470 So.2d 760 (1985); *Boynton v. Casey,* 543 F.Supp. 995 (1982); *Birdsey v. Grand Blanc Community Schools,* 344 N.W.2d 342 (1983) and *Pollnow v. Glennon,* 594 F.Supp. 220 (1984).
53. 842 F.2d 920, 924 (1988). The court reversed the district court's decision because new evidence was presented during the school board's closed deliberation, evidence that had not been presented during the open hearing. This was ruled to be a denial of procedural due process.
54. 864 F.2d 426, 429 (1988).
55. 500 So.2d 455 (1986).
56. 187 Cal. Rptr. 47; 654 P.2d 242; 33 C.3d 301 (1982); 187 Cal. Rptr. 472, 476 (1982).
57. *Id.* at 474.
58. 868 F.2d 90 (1989).
59. 645 F.Supp. 798, 805 (1986).
60. 426 F.Supp. 397 (1977); 583 F.2d 91 (1978).
61. 187 Cal. Rptr. 400 (1982).
62. *W.A.N. v. School Board of Polk County,* 504 So.2d (1987).
63. *Smith v. Dallas County Board of Education,* 480 F.Supp. 1324 (1979).
64. 676 F.Supp. 755 (1987).
65. 676 F.Supp. 752 (1987).

66. 423 F.Supp. 767 (1976).
67. 661 F.Supp. 155 (1987).
68. 661 F.Supp. 157 (1987).
69. 661 F.Supp. 159 (1987).
70. 477 So.2d 237 (1985).
71. *Id.* at 239.
72. *Id.* at 242.
73. *Id.* at 241.
74. *Id.* at 241.
75. 826 F.2d 526.
76. *Id.* at 529.
77. *Id.*
78. 474 F.Supp. 244 (1979); 644 F.2d 397; 564 F.Supp. 177 (1985).
79. 479 F.Supp. 244, 265.
80. *Id.*
81. *Id.*
82. 644 F.2d 397, 404.
83. *Id.* at 405.
84. *Id.* at 406.
85. 429 N.W.2d 607 (1988); 348 N.E.2d 299 (1976); 475 A.2d 289 (1984).
86. 479 A.2d 671 (1984).
87. 344 S.E.2d 633 (1986); 705 F.Supp. 870 (1988).
88. 211 N.J.Super. 54 (1985).
89. *Id.* at 58.
90. *Id.* at 62.
91. *Id.*
92. Simon, 1984, "Discipline in the Public Schools: A Dual Standard for Handicapped and Non-handicapped Students?" *Journal of Law Education* 13:209.
93. 108 S.Ct. 592 (1988).
94. *Id.* at 594.
95. *Id.* at 604.
96. *Id.* at 604.
97. *Id.* at 605.
98. *Id.* at 605.
99. *Id.* at 605.
100. *Id.* at 605.
101. Mizell, 1978, "Designing and Implementing Effective In-school Alternatives to Suspension," *Urban Review* 10:213.
102. *Id.* at 213.
103. *Id.* at 213, 214. He cited the Juvenile Justice and Delinquency Prevention Act of 1974, which included a Congressional finding stating that "Juvenile

delinquency can be prevented through programs to keep students in elementary and secondary schools through the prevention of unwarranted and arbitrary suspensions and expulsions.''

104. Radin, 1988, ''Alternatives to Suspension and Corporal Punishment,'' *Urban Education* 22: 476. Some of the studies reviewed by Radin are referenced in the descriptions of various types.

105. *Id.* at 481.

106. *Id.* at 487.

107. Zimmerman, and Archbold, 1979, ''On-Campus Suspension: What It is and Why It Works,'' *NASSP Bulletin* 63:63.

108. Keifer, 1980, ''An Inexpensive Alternative to Suspension,'' *NASSP Bulletin* 64:112.

109. Noblit and Short, 1985, ''Rhetoric and Reality in In-School Suspension Programs,'' *The High School Journal* 68:59.

110. *Id.*

111. *Id.*

112. *Id.* at 60.

113. *Id.*

114. Chapter 6, Article 1. Suspension or Expulsion sec. 48900 to 48925.

115. Clothing having the insignias of the Raiders and Kings, two professional sports teams, cannot be worn on some campuses because local gangs have adopted them as their badges of identity.

116. As one principal said, ''I know we studied it when I was taking school law but I don't remember what it said anymore.'' When asked what due process was required, however, his definition was legally correct.

117. The quality and effectiveness of this program depends on the staff working with the students. At the present time it is very successful.

SEARCHING STUDENTS TO
KEEP SCHOOLS SAFE:
THE NEED FOR ALTERNATIVES

Jacqueline Stefkovich

[B]ecause drug use and possession of weapons have become increasingly common among young people, an immediate response frequently is required not just to maintain an environment conducive to learning, but to protect the safety of students and school personnel. . . . government has a heightened obligation to safeguard students whom it compels to attend school.

—Justice Blackmun

For several decades, drugs and violence in our public schools have been major concerns of educators and policymakers alike. As early as 1978, the United States Department of Education released *Violent schools, safe schools: The safe school study report to congress* outlining problems of violence in schools.[1] With recent events such as the much-publicized killings of students in the New York City Public Schools, the issue of school violence and its counterpart, school safety, have taken on added dimensions and attracted renewed interest.[2]

Much of this interest focuses on schools as institutions and the interaction of schools with the legal system. This educational-legal juxtaposition has come about because issues of school violence are often associated with drugs and weapons brought into the schools.

One way that schools have reacted is to search students. Some school officials have searched all students, not merely those suspected of wrong-doing. A number of districts have installed metal detectors in their schools;[3] others have gone so far as to justify highly intrusive searches, such as strip searches in the name of safety.[4] Some of these approaches have resulted in litigation and in new examinations by the courts of issues of school violence and school safety, particularly as they relate to students' Fourth Amendment rights against unlawful searches and seizures.[5]

In *Williams by Williams v. Ellington* (1991), a 6th circuit court upheld the strip search of school students. This case marked the eleventh time that a student strip search had been litigated.[6] Since the first case was decided in 1973, no other court had been willing to uphold a search as intrusive as this one. The search was for drugs.

In *People v. Dukes* (1992), a New York state court became the first court to make legal the use of metal detectors in public schools. No other courts have yet addressed this issue.

Public school officials are finding themselves in a dilemma.[7] On one hand, they have a responsibility—both moral and legal—to keep the schools safe and to maintain a school climate that is conducive to learning. On the other hand, schools teach students that the United States Constitution protects individual rights. One of those rights, guaranteed by the Fourth Amendment and upheld in *New Jersey v. T.L.O.* (1985), is protection of students against unlawful searches and seizures.

This chapter is divided into three sections, each addressing a different aspect of the school search dilemma. Part 1 provides a legal analysis. It describes standards for conducting school searches, as set forth by the U.S. Supreme Court, and, in light of these standards, considers the legality of conducting highly intrusive searches or mass searches of students (e.g., with metal detectors) in public schools when there is a perception of danger in those schools.

Part 2 considers nonlegal aspects of school searches, namely the influence of the school's culture on the viability of conducting mass and intrusive searches. Here, I will discuss results from a study of the influence of factors such as the philosophy of the school, the school's leadership, and community relations on school search practices.

Part 3 discusses alternatives to conducting mass and intrusive searches. The premise underlying this discussion is that school officials may not have to make a decision between school safety and students' rights, there are both different ways of viewing the problem and different strategies for seeking a solution. These views and strategies are presented with respect to three models: a legal due process model, a mental health model, and a school reform model.

LEGAL IMPLICATIONS OF
SEARCHING STUDENTS

The following section discusses the legal implications of searching students in order to ensure safety in the public schools. It begins by describing standards for conducting school searches that were set forth by the Supreme Court in *New Jersey v. T.L.O.*[8] It then examines the legality of conducting mass and intrusive searches in public schools when there is a perception of danger in those schools. Cases such as the *Dukes* metal detector decision and the *Williams* strip search opinion are reviewed in light of what the *T.L.O.* court, and subsequent lower courts, did and did not say about the legality of such searches.

The Fourth Amendment to the United States Constitution guarantees that ''The right of the people to be secure in their persons, houses, paper, and effects, against unreasonable searches and seizures, shall not be violated, and no Warrants shall issue, but upon probable cause, supported by Oath or affirmation, and particularly describing the place to be searched, and the persons or things to be seized.''

The most important case to date on the authority of public school officials to conduct searches of students on school grounds is *New Jersey v. T.L.O.*, a landmark decision handed down by the Supreme Court on 15 January, 1985. The *T.L.O.* case dealt with the search of a student's purse for cigarettes in violation of a school rule. In looking for the cigarettes, the vice-principal who conducted the search found marijuana. The Supreme Court maintained that the search was legal.[9]

In rendering this opinion, the Court acknowledged that students in schools have Fourth Amendment rights, but balanced students' rights against school administrators' obligations to maintain order and discipline in the schools.[10] As a result of this decision, students' privacy rights in schools are afforded a lower standard of protection than is usually given to citizens.

Under traditional Fourth Amendment analysis, for a search to be legal, police officers must have ''probable cause to believe that a crime has been committed and that evidence of the crime will be found in the place to be searched.''[11] After *T.L.O.*, public school officials need only have a ''reasonable suspicion'' that a law or school rule has been violated.

The *T.L.O.* court established that the reasonable suspicion standard, which is far more lenient than the probable cause standard, is determined in two ways. First, the search must be justified at its inception. Second, the search must be reasonably related in scope to the circumstances that prompted the search. [12]

A search is justified at its inception when "there are reasonable grounds for suspecting that the search will turn up evidence that the student has violated or is violating either the law or the rules of the school." [13] A search is permissible in scope when "the measures adopted are reasonably related to the objectives of the search and not excessively intrusive in light of the age and sex of the student and the nature of the infraction." [14]

On one hand, the *T.L.O.* decision represented a major legal breakthrough in Fourth Amendment jurisprudence both by declaring that students have Fourth Amendment rights and by determining that students could be searched under a reasonable suspicion standard. On the other hand, *T.L.O.* was a relatively narrow decision dealing with a purse search. In this respect, it left unanswered several important legal questions whose resolve is essential to addressing problems of school safety and school violence.

Thus, while both the *Dukes* opinion, the first decision to uphold the use of metal detectors in the schools, and the *Williams* opinion, the first decision to uphold the legality of very intrusive strip searches in the schools, use the reasonable suspicion standard articulated in *T.L.O.*, the legality of the searches conducted in these cases hinge on two important legal issues left open by the *T.L.O.* decision. These issues include the need for individualized suspicion and applicability of the reasonable suspicion standard to searches more intrusive than the *T.L.O.* purse search.

Individualized Suspicion

In *People v. Dukes* (1992), the most prominent legal issue centered around searching students without individualized suspicion. Individualized suspicion is suspicion that a particular individual has engaged in misconduct or may be in possession of contraband or evidence of misconduct. Nonindividualized suspicion includes situations where misconduct is suspected, but the suspicion is directed at the student population in general, or a certain segment of the student population, rather than at a specific individual. [15]

For instance, metal detector searches of all students entering a school or the search of an entire class based on the belief that someone in the room has a weapon are examples of searches involving nonindividualized suspicion.

The need for individualized suspicion as a component of a reasonable suspicion was one of the issues left unanswered by the *T.L.O.* court. Because the search in the *T.L.O.* case involved individualized suspicion (i.e., the vice-principal was informed that T.L.O. was suspected of smoking), the Supreme Court maintained that it did not need to consider cases with nonindividualized suspicion. In this regard, the *T.L.O.* court specifically stated that it was not deciding the issue of whether or not individualized suspicion is an essential element of the reasonableness standard.[16]

While the Court stated that "the Fourth Amendment imposes no irreducible requirement of individualized suspicion,"[17] it also noted that "in other contexts this Court has determined that 'some quantum of individualized suspicion' is usually a prerequisite to a constitutional search or seizure."[18]

Finally, and probably most importantly for the issues discussed in this chapter, the *T.L.O.* court noted that "Exceptions to the requirement of individualized suspicion are generally appropriate where the privacy interests implicated by a search are minimal and where "other safeguards" are available "to assure that the individual's reasonable expectation of privacy is not "subject to the discretion of the official in the field.""''[19]

While the necessity of individualized suspicion as related to the reasonableness of searching school students has never reached the Supreme Court level, a number of lower courts have grappled with this issue.[20] These cases inevitably center around school safety issues, most notably, searching students for drugs and/or weapons.

With the exception of the *Dukes* opinion, lower courts have generally found that, unless there is some immediate danger, individualized suspicion is a necessary prerequisite to conducting mass searches. Two of the cases reported address the legality of searching students in connection with field trips. Here, even though the rationale administrators provided was that they feared students would bring drugs or alcohol on the trips, both a 6th circuit court, in *Webb v. McCullough*,[21] and the supreme court of the state of Washington, in *Kuehn v. Renton School District No. 403*, required individualized suspicion in order for the searches to be legal.

In the *Webb* case, a principal in charge of 140 students on a field trip to Hawaii had students' rooms searched after he was informed that the students may be violating school rules against possession of alcohol. The court denied summary judgment for the defendants maintaining that "The record does not reflect that the . . . search of Webb's room was other than random. Thus, if we look solely to the application of the guidelines provided by *T.L.O.* to the facts considered by the district court, it is possible that a jury would find that the search was unreasonable."[22]

In *Kuehn,* there was a policy that school officials would search all students' luggage as a precondition to the students' participation in a band concert tour. Even though the trip was not mandated, and despite the fact that the policy had been instituted because liquor had been found in students' rooms on previous trips, the court nonetheless maintained that the searches violated students' Fourth Amendment rights. Unlike the *Dukes* opinion, which justified mass searches in the name of safety, the *Kuehn* court maintained that these searches were not reasonable because they lacked individualized suspicion. As the court noted, "When school officials search large groups of students solely for the purpose of deterring disruptive conduct and without any suspicion of each individual searched, the search does not meet the reasonable belief standard."[23]

Another case, *Burnham v. West,* involved mass searches of middle school students for marijuana after the principal smelled the drug in a school hallway.[24] The court in this case declared the search to be unconstitutional but opened the door to a somewhat more lenient interpretation by stating that the outcome of the case might have been different if there had been an established prevalence of drug use in the school, if suspicion had been narrowed to a smaller group, or if there had been a more immediate problem.

In a later case, *In re Alexander B.,* the court used two of these possible exceptions—suspicion narrowed to a smaller group and response to an immediate problem—as the basis for upholding a search that lacked individualized suspicion.[25] In this case, an administrator acted to break up a clash between two groups of students known to be associated with different gangs in the neighborhood. During this altercation, an unidentified member of one group said, "Don't pick on us; one of those guys has a gun." A police officer standing nearby searched the members of this group, finding a machete knife and scabbard.

While the *Alexander* court acknowledged the importance of individualized suspicion, it distinguished this case from other mass searches noting that suspicion was focused on a group of five or six students, and, "given the potential danger that would have resulted from inaction," a weapons search of these students was reasonable.[26] In its reasoning, the court maintained that "the gravity of the danger posed by possession of a firearm or other weapon on campus was great compared to the relatively minor intrusion involved in investigating the veracity of the unidentified student's accusation against a handful of high-school-age boys."[27]

Thus, while lower courts, in general, have interpreted the reasonable suspicion standard as one that requires individualized suspicion, some courts have carved out exceptions to this rule. These courts have maintained that a search may be reasonable if the suspicion is narrowed to a small group of students, if there is immediate danger to others, or if there has been a history of problems.

The *Dukes* metal detector case seems to deviate from this line of reasoning in that it involved the search of a large number of students. Also, while there was a genuine concern for safety because students had been killed in other New York City schools, the search was not conducted in reaction to an immediate situation as in the *Alexander* case.[28] If anything, there might have been a history of problems in the school that the *Dukes* court failed to specify. Similar to the *Webb* and *Kuehn* cases, the school in *Dukes* used searching as a prevention strategy. However, unlike these "field trip" cases, the *Dukes* court clearly perceived a widespread, possibly imminent, danger. Thus, in upholding metal detector searches in the schools, the *Dukes* court noted that

> It is unfortunate that we have reached the point where so many of our great public institutions resemble medieval fortresses. This sight is a sobering reminder of the price we pay for security. But to envision students and teachers . . . huddled in fear as they attempt to go about their daily work is a far worse image.[29]

In addition, the *Dukes* court distinguishes this case from others in two significant ways. First, the search was a very nonintrusive administrative search. Second, the searches were conducted in accordance with very specific guidelines adopted by the school system.[30]

These guildelines provided advance notice to students that searches would be conducted, searched students randomly, and prescribed strict procedural requirements for the actual search itself (e.g., the scanning device should not touch the student's body); if the scanner is activated, the student is asked to remove all metal objects from his or her person and the scan is repeated; follow-up searches are conducted privately and by officials who are of the same sex as the student.[31]

Whether the *Dukes* decision reflects a trend away from applying the individualized suspicion requirement to school-related cases or whether metal detector cases are considered to be so unintrusive and the danger so great as to constitute another exception to the rule is yet to be seen. However, with increased concerns about violence in the schools and more reported use of metal detectors, we can be reasonably assured that the courts have not seen the last of such cases.

Intrusive Searches

In the *Williams* case, the issue at hand concerned the legality of conducting highly intrusive strip searches. While the *T.L.O.* court offered no definitive answer as to the standard for more intrusive searches, such as the strip search in the *Williams* case, legal commentators and lower courts have assumed, for the most part, that highly intrusive searches would have a difficult time conforming to the reasonableness standard.[32] Generally, the more intrusive the search, the greater the need for justification of that search.[33]

One basis for this conclusion lies in Justice Stevens's dissent in *T.L.O.* where he states that

> One thing is clear under any standard—the shocking strip searches that are described in some cases have no place in the schoolhouse. . . . To the extent that deeply intrusive searches are ever reasonable outside the custodial context, it surely must only be to prevent imminent and serious harm.[34]

This logic is also commensurate with that of an earlier case, *Doe v. Renfrow,* where the court acknowledged, "It does not require a constitutional scholar to conclude that a nude search of a 13-year-old child is an invasion of constitutional rights of some magnitude."[35]

The *Williams* opinion deviates from that of other lower courts in that it is the first decision to uphold a very intrusive strip search of a student in the public schools. In this case, a student suspected of possessing drugs was requested by a school official of the same sex to remove her T-shirt and to lower her blue jeans to her knees.

In its ruling for the defendant school district, the *Williams* court concluded that the search was reasonable in that it was performed in accordance with a valid district-wide policy. Explicitly citing the *T.L.O.* decision and the standards contained therein, this policy allowed for "the search of a pupil's person if there is a reasonable suspicion that the student is concealing evidence of an illegal activity."[36]

The *Williams* court maintained that this strip search was not in violation of the Fourth Amendment. It was reasonable at its inception because there had been a great deal of evidence indicating that Ms. Williams had drugs in her possession, including a tip from a fellow student, suspicions voiced by the student's father to school authorities, an incriminating letter found in the student's typing class, and reports from her teacher of odd behavior on the day of the search.

The court also reasoned that the scope of the search was justified because the student was suspected of carrying a small glass vial containing a white, powdery substance believed to be illicit drugs. Thus, the vial was small enough to be hidden under the student's clothing. In addition, the vial was not found in the student's locker or in her purse as the result of searches conducted immediately prior to the strip search.

While the *Williams* case may be distinguished from other strip search cases based on the "totality of the circumstances,"[37] which included both quality and quantity of information, it remains a troubling decision.

This decision is troubling for several reasons. First, it provides little guidance for determining how much evidence is enough to justify a strip search. If the school principal had had a little less information or a little less reliable information, would the search have still been reasonable? This decision will need to be left up to future courts who, unfortunately, in the face of increased reports of drugs in the schools, will likely be forced to deal with this issue.

Second, as mentioned previously, this is the first time that a court has upheld a strip search as intrusive as this one in the public schools. The fear is that future courts will follow the same trend or, worse yet, that some school officials will use this decision to justify other, perhaps less reasonable, strip searches.

Finally, the *Williams* decision, which upholds intrusive searches, combined with the *Dukes* decision, which justifies mass searches without individualized suspicion, may be the harbinger of new legal standards for school searches, standards that greatly diminish Fourth Amendment protections for students in schools. In this sense, Justice Brennan may have been right when he noted that use of a "balancing test" (i.e., the privacy rights of students balanced against school officials' obligation to maintain order and discipline in the schools) "portends a dangerous weakening of the purpose of the Fourth Amendment to protect the privacy and security of our citizens."[38]

SCHOOL SEARCHES AND SCHOOL CULTURE

Recognizing that the legal system provides an incomplete, at best, answer to the school search dilemma, I consider in this section the viability of school searches in light of their relationship to the culture of the school. After providing a definition of—and some brief background information on—school culture, the major part of this discussion will focus on a study I conducted describing the influence of cultural factors such as the philosophy of the school, the school's leadership, and community relations on school search policies and practices.

Shortly after the Supreme Court handed down its opinion in the *T.L.O.* case, Ellen Goodman, a columnist for the *Boston Globe*, speculated that this decision "would make little difference in the every day running of the schools." As Ms. Goodman noted,

Many schools already operate like communities based on mutual respect, others have the atmosphere of a 19th century workhouse. . . . [I]t should be noted that the Supreme Court didn't make a decision in the literal sense of that word. The Supreme Court hasn't resolved our conflicts about safety and privacy or about the relationship of students to the schools. It has merely reflected and perhaps heightened our ambivalence.[39]

This ambivalence about safety, privacy, and students' relationships to the schools is clearly illustrated in the different ways the justices approached the school search dilemma. For instance, Justice Powell, in his concurring opinion in *T.L.O.*, noted that because of "the special characteristics" of elementary and secondary schools, students should have a lesser expectation of privacy than other members of the population. "Without first establishing discipline and maintaining order, teachers cannot begin to educate their students."[40]

Justice Stevens, however, observed that:

Schools are places where we inculcate the values essential to the meaningful exercise of rights and responsibilities by self-governing citizenry. If the nation's students can be convicted through the use of arbitrary methods destructive of personal liberty, they cannot help but feel they have been dealt with unfairly.[41]

Issues of school culture lie at the very heart of those arguments posed by Justices Powell and Stevens and in Goodman's observation that "Many schools already operate like communities based on mutual respect, others have the atmosphere of a 19th century workhouse." Thus, while case law is a major factor in deciding if school officials *may* search students and the types of searches they *may* conduct, it is likely that the culture of a school will wield as much or more influence in determining whether or not the school official *will* search.

The culture of a school describes the way things are by interpreting and giving meaning to events, behaviors, words, and acts. It also prescribes the way people should act according to the norms of the institution. Hence, the culture of the school regulates appropriate and acceptable behavior in given situations and, consequently, defines what is true and good.[42] Given these characteristics, school culture has been defined as "socially shared and transmitted knowledge of what is, and what ought to be, symbolized in act and artifact."[43]

In view of somewhat ambiguous legal constructs, this concept of culture may account for the presence or absence of mass or intrusive searches in schools regardless of the legality of the search. Thus, factors related to the culture of the school may provide important nonlegal reasons why searches are or are not conducted in schools.

In an indepth study of search policies and practices in three New Jersey high schools, conducted ten months after the *T.L.O.* decision, I found that searches had not increased after the Supreme Court's ruling and that, indeed, the schools conducted few searches of any kind, including mass searches or highly intrusive searches.[44]

In this research, I identified a variety of nonlegal factors that influenced search policies and practices, which coincided with some of the same factors that Lightfoot experienced in her research on high schools, factors that are directly related to the culture of the school.[45] These factors include the philosophy of the school, its leadership, and community expectations.

While the scope of this chapter is not nearly so large as to describe the New Jersey study in detail, some of the findings of this study do shed a great deal of light on the influence of school culture on search policies and practices. The most pertinent of these findings are included in the descriptions below.

School Philosophies

While the three schools in my study were quite different demographically, they shared similar philosophies toward students, philosophies that emphasized respect for individuals. This type of philosophy was dramatically illustrated in the words of the board president in Lincoln, a wealthy suburban school.

When asked why there were so few searches in Lincoln, she stated,

In part, it goes along with the philosophy that people work best in a surrounding where they are respected. . . . The entire school system, even in the grade schools, has a respect for the rights of others and for their individuality. So you try not to infringe on that individuality.''

Also illustrative of this point is an excerpt from the school handbook in Garden City, a large, ethnically diverse urban school. It states that

Any philosophy of education must emphasize the fulfillment of the individual within a democratic process. In a world that is continually changing, the school environment must reflect the atmosphere conducive to cooperative endeavors involving students, teachers, and administrators. Through the cooperation of home and community, each individual can aspire to attain maximum benefit.[46]

This attitude also prevailed in Indian River, a small, mostly white, rural district. Here, students were seen as partners in the educational experience of the school. The philosophy statement in the student handbook read: "Lines of communication are maintained in order to insure an understanding of the needs and desires of each group."[47]

While having these statements in the student handbook and in the philosophy of the school do not, by themselves, prove a nonadversarial relationship between students and school officials, what was so special about these schools was that the staff members actually held these beliefs themselves.

This attitude was reflected in numerous remarks similar to those of the board president in Lincoln, in the administrators' handling of school searches (which is described in more detail later), and in a genuine concern and respect for students' rights, which students recognized. As one student in Garden City pointed out, "If you are doing what you are supposed to be doing, you aren't bothered. . . . [The administrators] won't just stop you in the middle of the hall to pat you down. They'd take you into the office and ask you what was going on."

School Leadership

The attitudes and approach of the leadership of the schools also influenced search policies and practices. When asked why they had not conducted greater numbers of searches or more intrusive searches, administrators expressed great sensitivity for the privacy rights of students.

Illustrative of this point were the reactions of Garden City's Assistant Housemaster (and disciplinarian) who, when asked about personal searches, explained, "[When I search students], I have no doubt in my mind that they were doing something [wrong]. In most cases, the physical evidence of that marijuana cigarette that the group was smoking is present."

The only departures from this procedure came in the event of immediate danger to the students. The Assistant Housemaster described these types of situations in the following manner:

The only other times [that I search] are times like when a student comes up to me and says, "I was just in the hallway and this kid came up to me and pulled a knife out on me and wanted. . . ." Those kinds of things I would act on right away. Maybe I act on them because it would be just like my son or daughter.

You can't take these things for granted and say, "They're not going to bother you" or anything like that because, God forbid, that the kid would go and stab another student or something. On cases like that, that's probably the only time that I'm not sure, that I have to investigate it. But, even then, the student has specifically mentioned another student as the one who has threatened him.

Similarly, in the rural district that I studied, the superintendent of schools noted, "We are scrupulous in protecting the rights of our students here at Indian River."

Others also seemed to feel that the administrators were sincere in their pro-student rights attitudes. As one teacher observed, "I think the administration here cares too much for the kids [to conduct mass searches]." Accordingly, a student noted,

> Generally, the administration here tries to get along with the students. The principal doesn't want to search a lot. It would take too much of his time and it would cause too much friction with the students. . . . He's got something good going with the students. There's a general understanding. Even the vice-principal is that way. He's in charge of discipline. People go in and even after they get punished, they think he is fair.

Perhaps most telling, however, was the reaction of Lincoln's principal who asked increduously: "Why would we conduct [mass] searches? . . . It would just make the students think that we are suspicious of them."

Community Influence

Dolbeare and Hammond, in their seminal study on the implementation of *Abington v. Schempp,* the United States Supreme Court's decision banning school prayer, found that community interests and concerns go far in shaping the policies and practices of the schools in that community and, oftentimes, wield a greater influence than the actual court decisions.[48] These were also the findings of my study of school search and seizure policies in the wake of the *T.L.O.* decision. I discovered that how the community (i.e., school board members, parents) reacted to the idea of mass or intrusive searches or how school personnel perceived community reactions were important factors in determining whether or not these types of searches were conducted.

For example, several individuals in Indian River stated that the school would not conduct intrusive or mass searches out of fear of being sued. One teacher directly linked this fear of litigation to concerns about community disapproval. As she noted, "We're not going to be taken to court. There's always that threat. It doesn't look good for anybody to be taken to court and to have your position challenged in the community and in the school."

In Garden City, there was a widespread perception among the staff that the parents and students of the school have a great deal of accessibility to local government and, hence, to the mayor-appointed school board. As the school social worker noted, "there's a sense of accessibility to town government. . . . it's more like it is in a smaller town than in a large city. Another staff member was even more blunt: "It's nothing for students or parents who are unhappy with the way the school has treated them to go directly to the mayor if they know him or to a school board member rather than confronting the administrator or teacher." One Garden City board member who felt that her comments were representative of the entire board, stated that "An administrator has no business in a student's purse or in the students' bathrooms unless he has reason to believe that something is really going on in there. There must be a really *specific* reason."

There were similar reactions in Lincoln, a wealthy school with an active Parent-Teacher-Student organization. Here, parents were very vocal about the running of the school and had persuaded the administration to back down on a proposed policy requiring all school news articles to be approved by the principal prior to publication. As one student noted, "I'm sure that my mother would complain [if there were a lot of searches]. She complains about other things [that are school-related]." The attitude was echoed by the president of the PTSO who claimed that "Parents would be incensed if there were massive locker searches." This was a powerful pro-student rights statement considering that staff and students alike saw lockers as "school property" and locker searches as only mildly intrusive, or as one student put it, "not a real search."

This combination of close contacts between the school board and students and parents, coupled with a pro-student rights attitude on the part of the board, appeared to be a factor in deterring school officials from conducting more numerous or more intrusive student searches.

ALTERNATIVES TO MASS AND INTRUSIVE SEARCHING

School officials may not have to make a decision between school safety and students' rights. There are both alternative ways of viewing the problem and alternative strategies for seeking a solution. This section identifies and presents a brief description of three models that school officials may use in seeking alternative solutions to conducting mass and intrusive searches. Advantages and disadvantages of each approach are discussed. These alternatives include a legal due process model, a mental health model, and a school reform model.

These particular models spring from the research in parts one and two of this chapter and from related literature in the areas of school administration and school improvement. They are not meant to be inclusive, but

but are merely representative of various approaches that might be considered. In addition, the aim of this section is to provide an overview rather than a comprehensive discussion of these models.

A Legal Due Process Model

School officials may consider adoption of a due process model in order to safeguard students' rights and keep mass and intrusive searches at a minimum. The conceptual basis underlying this approach is rational and legalistic. In organizational terms, this conception is probably closest to what theorists categorize as a structural framework (i.e., one that focuses on goals, policies, rules and hierarchies).[49]

An underlying premise behind this model is that school safety and violence are essentially legal problems and that searches are an appropriate way to address these concerns as long as students are given advance notice and the searches themselves are legally permissible. Mass and intrusive searches would be allowed only under certain narrowly tailored circumstances as defined by state statutes or case law.

Driving this model is the development of strong, clearly defined search-and-seizure policies and guidelines that stress procedural safeguards and are written and made readily available to students, probably through the student handbook of the school.

These guidelines would likely contain some of the same safeguards that I discovered in my research in three high schools. They include, but are not limited to, emphasizing less intrusive searches, such as locker searches; asking consent of the students; and having a witness at each search. Personal searches, such as patdowns, or searches of purses and pockets would be conducted by school officials of the same sex as the student searched.

The advantage of the legal due process model is its simplicity. It is logical, straightforward, clean, and easy to implement. In addition, if the policies and guidelines are developed carefully, and with the advice of legal counsel, and if they are carried out properly, they stand a good chance, if challenged, of being upheld by the courts. Even in cases as controversial as *Dukes* and *Williams,* the courts took notice of the existence of search guidelines.

For example, the *Williams* court found that the school district was not liable for damages because the search had been conducted in accordance with what it (the court) considered to be a constitutionally valid policy and because there was no history that the policy had been "repeatedly or even sporadically misapplied by school officials in the past."[50] This policy was based on standards set forth in the *T.L.O.* decision.

On a similar note, the *Dukes* court stated that ''By adopting the guidelines, the Board of Education has taken a significant step in the battle to maintain peace and serenity in our schools. For recognizing the problem and seeking to address it in a responsible manner, the Board deserves our support and respect.''[51]

While there is much to be said for this model, it also carries with it serious limitations. First, this legal due process approach fails to take into account the complexity of schools as organizations. It assumes that schools are logical, rational institutions. Some researchers have challenged this presumption outright.[52] Others acknowledge that, on one level, schools may operate within a rational, structural framework, but they are also influenced, perhaps even more so, by politics and symbolism.[53]

Second, this model assumes an adversarial role between school official and student, a role that is not necessarily the case. As Justice Powell noted in his concurring opinion in *T.L.O.*,

> The special relationship between teacher and student . . . distinguishes the setting within which school children operate. Law enforcement officers function as adversaries of criminal suspects. These officers have the responsibility to investigate criminal activity, to locate and arrest those who violate our laws, and to facilitate the charging and bringing of such persons to trial. Rarely does this type of adversarial relationshp exist between school authorities and pupils.[54]

This observation is also in concert with my findings that school authorities are concerned with the welfare of students and, indeed, value students' individual rights.

A third weakness, and one closely aligned to the adversarial concepts described above, is that this model is based on a theory of retribution.[55] There are rules. The rules are made clear. Those who violate the rules are punished. Unlike the teacher in Indian River, who noted, ''We would like to clean up drug use completely, not so much in terms of punishment, but to get kids help,'' this model, standing alone, leaves little room for the kinds of assistance and treatment that students may need as they develop into young adults.[56]

A Mental Health Model

Another alternative to mass and intrusive searching of students involves applying a mental health model to the student violence problem. The conceptual basis for this model derives from a mixture of the classic medical model of psychology, which aims at prevention, diagnosis, treatment, and rehabilitation, and sociologically based theories that call attention to the importance of familial influences on student behavior. The underlying premise behind this model is that drug abuse and violence are, first and foremost, mental health problems (rather than legal problems). Therefore, this approach places a heavy emphasis on early identification of problems, counseling, and intervention techniques.

An example of this type of approach was apparent in Indian River where if a student is acting strangely in class, the procedure is to send the student to the school nurse rather than to the disciplinarian. As one teacher in that school noted,

> As long as students aren't disruptive, you can't accuse them outright .. . . because in our school, there's a procedure [with] suspected drugs or suspected alcohol abuse. There's a teacher that you refer them to. It's a counseling situation, an attempt to get them away from it. They've had a couple of good referrals. One girl, we actually got out of the building to Florida for rehabilitation for a whole year. She's back with us now and she's functioning very well.

Similar procedures and programs were in place in Garden City in Lincoln. Both of these schools stressed rehabilitation, and Lincoln had instituted a nationally recognized peer-counseling program aimed at drug and alcohol abuse. This program stressed "rehabilitative and educational" efforts to combat drug and alcohol use.

The strength of the mental health model is that it strikes at the heart of school violence problems. In contrast to the legal due process approach, which attacks only the symptoms of school violence, the mental health model considers causes. This model is probably more in concert with the nonadversarial culture of many school. As Justices Powell and O'Connor observed, school officials often possess an attitude of "personal responsibility for the student's welfare as well as for his education."[57]

A major weakness of this model is that, taken alone, it places the burden of responsibility for the problem on the student (or perhaps on his or her family). It fails to recognize that there may be something about the culture of the school itself, or of the larger community, that may contribute to, or help assuage, the incidences of violence. In addition, tackling problems as large as drug abuse and violence requires a great deal of manpower and money. It is difficult for the schools alone, with their limited financial resources, to make a difference.

A School Reform Model

A third alternative to mass and intrusive searches is based on the school reform movement and, more specifically, on school restructuring.

Corbett has defined school restructuring as a rethinking of the fundamental structures of education that involves "alterations in a school district's pattern of rules, roles, relationships, and results."[58]

Restructuring springs from a vast array of school-improvement research conducted in the 1980s and a nationally recognized need for school improvement and school reform.[59] Corbett's definition drives from sociology; however, the theoretical underpinnings of restructuring vary according to the background and approach of individual researchers. Consequently, restructuring may also be grounded in other disciplines, such as psychology, anthropology, and political science.

While the school-restructuring movement has yet to focus on student rights, certain aspects of restructuring and some "restructured" schools provide many interesting alternatives to mass and intrusive searches. Two of these are mentioned below.

One alternative lies in the concept of a democratic school. Here, students take an active role in establishing guidelines and policies and in mediating discipline problems. Some researchers who advocate this approach have cited the National Institute of Education's study *Violent Schools, Safe Schools.*[60] In this report, findings indicated that there were higher rates of crime and violence in schools where students perceived that they had no internal control and could not influence what happened to them. Advocates of democratic schools believe that this approach gives students that sense of internal control.[61]

Changes in school roles and relationships also often include greater community involvement in the schools. As I noted in my study, community involvement strongly influenced the search policies and practices of the schools and, consequently, affected the rights of students. Accordingly, in the *Ingraham* decision, the Supreme Court observed that "the openness of the public school and its supervision by the community" may afford significant safeguards against the violation of constitutional rights.[62] School restructuring provides a vehicle for accomplishing this goal by opening the schools up to the community and actively involving the community in school decision making.

The school restructuring model, as it pertains to alternatives to school searching, has several strengths and advantages over the other models. Unlike the legal due process approach, the school reform model portrays schools as nonadversarial. In some schools, such as those depicted in the New Jersey study, this nonadversarial role is much more in keeping with the culture of the school. As Goldberg and Lynch point out, "Legal rules are developed in a culture different than that of education."[63] Hence, these authors purport that school reform through restructuring is both more humane and better able to meet the educational needs of students than an adversarial, procedurally driven approach. In addition, the school reform model stresses use of community resources and facilities. This sharing of resources has the potential to make up for some of the services lacking in the mental health model.

The weaknesses of the school reform model often lie in the readiness of a district for the extensive kinds of change that such a model implies. In short, if school districts take seriously Corbett's definition of restructuring (or similar definitions), school restructuring will take a great deal of time and planning.[64] This time commitment, coupled with the fact that restructuring is a fairly new concept, means that the ultimate success of such a plan has been largely unproven. This is not to say that school restructuring cannot or will not work, just that it may be too early to tell, and its success and degree of implementation may vary greatly depending upon cultural factors within the school district.

SUMMARY AND CONCLUSIONS

Violence has been a problem in our schools for several decades. With reports of recent killings in the school, this problem of violence has peaked a renewed interest both on the part of school officials and from the courts. Some school officials have taken drastic actions to keep their students safe. They have conducted mass searches of students with metal detectors and have even strip searched students for drugs. A few courts have even upheld such practices.

With at least some courts apparently condoning such practices in the name of safety, school administrators are left in a dilemma. First, these decisions have muddied the waters surrounding issues of when and under what circumstances school officials may conduct mass and/or intrusive searches of students. Second, school officials are caught in a bind. On the one hand, they want to keep their schools safe and maintain a climate conducive to learning. On the other hand, they teach their students that they have rights, among them the right to be free from unreasonable searches and seizures.

This chapter has considered this dilemma from three perspectives. First, it provided a legal analysis and attempted to clarify the conditions under which intrusive and mass searches are legally permissible. It concluded that such searches may be reasonable if there is an immediate danger to others or a history of problems in the school. In addition, mass searches may be justified if the danger is great and the search is minimally intrusive.

Second, the chapter looked at research conducted in three schools that chose not to conduct mass and intrusive searches and examined characteristics of the culture in these schools that served to curtail or prohibit such searching. Here, I concluded that, even if school officials may legally search, conditions in the school such as school leadership, philosophies, and community reactions often determine whether or not the official will search.

Finally, this chapter presented three alternative models to mass and intrusive searching. They included a legal due process model based on rules and procedures, a mental health model focusing on counseling and intervention techniques, and a school reform model that emphasized a fundamental change in the rules, roles, relationships, and results in restructured school districts.

While all these models have their unique strengths, they also have weaknesses. Consequently, none stands alone as "the answer" for all schools. A human resource model may work better in one district that has a great deal of resources and a philosophy, leadership, and community that supports counseling and intervention techniques, while another district might need to restructure its entire system. In addition, some districts may choose to combine models. For instance, they might begin with a legal due process model, but restructure their schools to have students participate in the rule-making, or they might combine the legal model with a mental health model.

However the particulars are worked out, these models do provide alternatives to mass and intrusive searches and, in some important ways, are able to address the school official's dilemma of providing a safe school that respects students' rights.

NOTES

1. National Institute of Education, U.S. Dept. of Health, Education, and Welfare, 1978, *Violent schools, safe schools: The safe school study report to Congress. (Wash. D.C.).*
2. J. Berger, 1992, *Bitter debate on scanning for firearms, New York Times*, 27 Feb. B2.
3. D. Harrington-Lueker, 1992, *Metal detectors, American School Board Journal 179:26. The National School Safety Center reports that approximately one-fourth of the country's big city schools use metal detectors to stem the flow of weapons in their schools.*
4. See, e.g., *Williams by Williams v. Ellington*, 936 F.2d 881 (6th Cir, 1991). In this case, a student was strip searched for drugs.
5. The Fourth Amendment to the United States Constitution guarantees "The right of the people to be secure in their persons, houses, paper, and effects, against unreasonable searches and seizures, shall not be violated, and no

Warrants shall issue, but upon probable cause, supported by Oath or affirmation, and particularly describing the place to be searched, and the persons or things to be seized.''

6. P. F. First, and L. F. Rossow, 1992, Introduction and comment, 34 *School Law Reporter* 34:1.

7. This paper addresses only the rights of public school students. Protections afforded under the United States Constitution apply to unlawful interference from government officials. Only in public schools are school officials seen as government agents. Consequently, students in nonpublic schools are not protected by the United States Constitution against school officials' actions.

8. T.L.O. are the initials of the student who was searched in this case. Because she was a minor at the time of the incident, her initials were used to protect her identity.

9. *New Jersey v. T.L.O.*, 317–18.

10. *New Jersey v. T.L.O.*, 339–40.

11. *Beck v. Ohio*, 379 U.S. 89 (1964); *Brinegar v. Unites States*, 338 U.S. 160 (1949).

12. *New Jersey v. T.L.O.*, 341.

13. *New Jersey v. T.L.O.*, 342.

14. *New Jersey v. T.L.O.*, 342.

15. M. Schreck, 1991, *The fourth amendment in the public schools: issues for the 1990's and beyond.* Hand-out distributed at the National Organization on Legal Problems of Education (NOLPE) Annual Conference. (On file with author at the University of Idaho College of Law.)

16. *New Jersey v. T.L.O.*, 342, n.8.

17. *New Jersey v. T.L.O.*, 342, n.8. The court is quoting *United States v. Martinez-Fuerte*, 428 U.S. 543, 560–61. (1976). See also, *Camara v. Municipal Court*, 387 U.S. 523 (1967).

18. *New Jersey v. T.L.O.*, 342.

19. *New Jersey v. T.L.O.*, 342. The court is quoting *Delaware v. Prouse*, 440 U.S. 648, 654–55 (1979).

20. See, e.g., *People v. Dukes*, 580 N.Y.S.2d 850 (1982), which examined the mass search of students with metal detectors for weapons, and *Kuehn v. Renton School District*, 694 P.2d 1078 (Wash. 1985), which examined the search of students' luggage for drugs and alcohol prior to a field trip.

21. *Webb v. McCullough*, 828 F.2d 1151 (1987).

22. *Webb v. McCullough*, 1156.

23. *Kuehn v. Renton School District*, 1079.

24. *Burnham v. West*, 681 F.Supp. 1169 (E.D. Va. 1988).

25. *In re Alexander B.*, 270 Cal. Rptr. 342 (1990).

26. *In re Alexander B.*, 344.

27. *In re Alexander B.*, 344.

28. *People v. Dukes*, 853. The court mentions New York City school records, which revealed that over 2,000 weapons were recovered in 1990–1991 and that there had been a recent fatal shooting in a Brooklyn school; however, the court does not make any conclusions, or cite statistics, regarding the particular school where the search occurred.

29. *People v. Dukes*, 853.

30. *People v. Dukes*, 851.

31. *People v. Dukes*, 851.

32. See, for example, C. W. Avery, and R. J. Simpson, 1987, Search and seizure: A risk assessment model for public school officials, *Journal of law and education* 16:403, 412, which noted that strip searches are extremely difficult to justify in a school setting. See also L. Bartlett, 1985, *New Jersey v. T.L.O.:* Not an end to school search litigation or commentaries, ED. L. REP. 23:801, which noted that five federal courts have ruled that strip searches are illegal without a warrant or probable cause.

33. Avery and Simpson, 403, 415.

34. *New Jersey v. T.L.O.*, 382, n.25.

35. *Doe v. Renfrow*, 631 F.2d 91 (7th Cir. 1980), *cert. denied*, 451 U.S. 1022 (1981), 92–93.

36. *Williams by Williams v. Ellington*, 884.

37. *Williams by Williams v. Ellington*, 889.

38. *New Jersey v. T.L.O.*, 358.

39. E. Goodman, 1985, Ambivalent about searches, *Boston Globe*, 22 Jan., 15.

40. *New Jersey v. T.L.O.*, 352.

41. *New Jersey v. T.L.O.*, 373–74.

42. G. B. Rossman, H. K. Corbett, and W. A. Firestone, 1988, *Change and effectiveness in schools: A cultural perspective* 5 Albany: SUNY Press.

43. E. K. Wilson, 1971, Quoted in Rossman et al., *Sociology: Rules, roles, & relationships*, 90.

44. J. A. Stefkovich, 1986, The influence on New Jersey public high schools of the U.S. Supreme Court's decision in *New Jersey v. T.L.O.* (1986) (ED.D. diss., Harvard University), 164–67.

45. S. L. Lightfoot, The good high school: portraits of character and culture. New York: Basic Books.

46. Cited in Stefkovich, 99.

47. Cited in Stefkovich, 150.

48. K. Dolbeare, and P. E. Hammond, 1971, *The school prayer decisions: From court policy to local practice*, 100–29, Chicago: Univ. Chicago Press.

49. L. J. Bolman, and T. E. Deal, 1984, *Modern approaches to understanding organizations* 31–35. San Francisco: Jossey-Bass.

50. *Williams by Williams v. Ellington*, 884–85.

51. *People v. Dukes*, 853.

52. L. Patterson, C. Purkey, and V. Parker, 1986, *Productive schools for a non-rational world,* 7–9, Alexandria, VA: Association for Supervision and Curriculum Development.
53. L. G. Bolman, T. E. Deal, 1991, The National Center for Educational Leadership, Occasional Paper No. 7, in *Images of leadership* Cambridge, MA: The National Center for Educational Leadership.
54. *New Jersey v. T.L.O.,* 319.
55. S. H. Kadish, S. J. Schulhofer, and M. G. Paulsen, 1983, *Criminal law and its processes,* 4th ed., 187–95 Boston, MA: Little, Brown.
56. Kadish, 195–210. According to this model, the person is punished solely in retaliation for having committed the offense. This is contrasted to models that punish for deterrence or to rehabilitate.
57. *New Jersey v. T.L.O.,* at 349–50.
58. H. D. Corbett, 1990, *On the meaning of restructuring* 2, Philadelphia: Research for Better Schools.
59. This line of research began with *A Nation at Risk,* a 1982 report that stated that "If an unfriendly foreign power had attempted to impose on America the mediocre educational performance that exists today, we might well have viewed it as an act of war. As it stands, we have allowed this to happen to ourselves." *A Nation at Risk: The Imperative for Educational Reform,* (The National Committee for Excellence in Education), 5, Washington, D.C.: U.S. Dept. of Education.
60. M. A. Hepburn, 1983, Can schools, teachers, and administrators make a difference? The research evidence, in *Democratic Education in Schools and Classrooms,* ed. M. A. Hepburn, National Council for the Social Studies Bulletin No. 70. Washington, D.C.
61. Hepburn, 11. See also, Kohlberg, 1981, *The philosophy of moral development: moral stages and the idea of justice,* San Francisco: Harper and Row. Where the author advocates democratic schools in response to his theory of "just communities" and the moral development of students.
62. *Ingraham v. Wright,* 430 U.S. 651 (1977), 670, quoted in *New Jersey v. T.L.O.,* 349.
63. S. S. Goldberg, and K. K. Lynch, 1992, Reconsidering the legalization of school reform: A case for implementing change through mediation, *Ohio state journal on dispute resolution,* vol. 7, no. 2, 199–215.
64. Corbett, 2.

TITLE IX: ARE WE MOVING FROM SEPARATE AND SORT OF EQUAL TO INTEGRATED AND UNEQUAL?
PERCEPTIONS OF TITLE IX COORDINATORS ON THE IMPACT OF TWENTY YEARS OF LEGISLATION

Katherine Hanson

> *No person in the United States shall, on the basis of sex, be excluded from participation in, be denied the benefits of, or be subjected to discrimination under any education program or activity receiving Federal financial assistance.*

With this crucial statement, Title IX of the Education Amendments of 1972 ushered in an era of restructuring that would have significant direct effects on one-half of the population of the United States—women and girls. Additionally, Title IX, with its mandate of nondiscrimination on the basis of sex, opened the doors for important changes for males as well. Twenty years ago Title IX was passed because Congress recognized that there was massive discrimination against girls and women by schools and colleges.

While Title IX has been on the books for twenty years, its impact has been both supported and devalued by various federal-level efforts. Initially, the regulations were backed up by intensive monitoring by the Department of Education's Office of Civil Rights (OCR). However, the broad coverage of the law was challenged by the Justice Department, and the enforcement of Title IX weakened within OCR.[1] With *Grove City College v. Bell,* the U.S. Supreme Court ruled that Title IX was program specific—only those programs and activities receiving direct federal funds needed to comply. Additionally, those categorical grant programs that support the implementation of Title IX—Women's Educational Equity Act (WEEA) and Title VI of the Civil Rights Act—continue to face drastic reductions. For instance, in the 1992 budget, WEEA had only a $500,000 allocation designated to the publishing activities, with no funding for new field-based grants.

In 1988 Congress enacted the Civil Rights Restoration Act "to restore . . . broad, institution-wide application" of civil rights laws, including Title IX. This was especially important since it restored the perspective that all parts of a school system or college that received federal education funds must comply with the law.

Most recently, the 1992 *Franklin v. Gwinnett County County (GA) Public Schools* ruling about the utility of Title IX as the basis for sexual harassment suits by students seems to further strengthen the impact of the legislation.[2] In this case, a female student sued her school district in federal court, claiming it did not protect her from sexual harassment by a teacher. Earlier suits had been dismissed because the judge ruled she could not collect damages under Title IX. However, the Supreme Court ruled—for the first time—that compensatory damages were allowed under Title IX. Since the courts ruled that litigants can sue for monetary damages under Title IX, it is likely that schools will pay increasing attention to the equitable education of their female students, especially as the ruling was not restricted to issues of sexual harassment but to Title IX in general.[3]

TITLE IX COVERAGE

The original Title IX regulations, issued in 1975, cover almost every aspect of education: admission to institutions; treatment of students in programs, courses, and other activities and services; and employment. The regulations covered both students and adults and were further strengthened under the Civil Rights Restoration Act in 1988.

Any school or college that receives federal education funds is required to comply with Title IX, including kindergartens, elementary and secondary schools, vocational schools, junior and community colleges, four-year colleges, universities, and graduate and professional schools. Pell grants are considered federal assistance and so bring any higher education institution into the compliance requirements. Any public or private institution that accepts federal education funds must comply with Title IX. Additionally, state and local governments, profit and nonprofit groups, and other organizations that accept federal education funds are covered by Title IX.

While Title IX has some exemptions, they tend to be rather narrow. For instance, schools can receive a religious exemption—if they are controlled by (not just affiliated with) religious organizations. Such waivers, granted by OCR, apply only to the specific part or parts of the regulation that conflict with the school's religious tenets. Such exemptions are not blanket exemptions and are designed to address those issues such as preparation for a specific religious function, such as the priesthood.

Another Title IX exemption is for sex education classes. The regulation permits "portions of classes in elementary and secondary schools which deal exclusively with human sexuality" to be sex-segregated. This narrow definition allows teachers to teach only that portion of a larger class curriculum that specifically deals with sexuality to have the option of teaching the boys and girls separately.

Another important exemption covers those schools attempting voluntary affirmative action to overcome previous discrimination or limited participation by one sex or the other. This would enable schools to provide special programs for girls who have traditionally been underserved. For instance, voluntary affirmative action would cover the provision of sports medicine services for females in order to bring them to the same level as services for males. Or, if a program has historically underserved males, affirmative action efforts to reach this population are encouranged by Title IX.

ENFORCEMENT OF TITLE IX

The major responsibility for enforcing Title IX belongs to the Office for Civil Rights within the U.S. Department of Education. As with Title VI of the Civil Rights Act, Title IX carries with it legal sanctions for noncompliance. The government can delay awarding funds, revoke awards, or bar institutions from eligibility for future awards. Additionally, the Justice Department may bring suit on behalf of the Department of Education.

Individuals who believe an institution has discriminated against them can file a complaint with OCR, which then investigates the complaint and attempts to resolve the problem through informal mediations. If this fails, OCR can either hold formal hearings or refer the case to the Justice Department for court action. If discrimination is found, the institution's federal funds can be terminated. Additionally, individuals have a private right to sue for discrimination. They can sue the schools directly, circumventing the federal procedures.

The penalties for discrimination are severe. But the regulations require that the government first attempt to resolve any discrimination problems through informal conciliation and persuasion. In the twenty years Title IX has been in force, no federal funds have ever been terminated on the grounds that a school has discriminated against its students on the basis of sex.[4]

IMPLICATIONS OF TITLE IX

Over the past twenty years, Title IX has provided the impetus for significant change within education and therefore within the larger society. For those who were in schools prior to 1972, there are the memories of sex-segregated classes, denial of admissions to vocational education classes, lack of access to advanced mathematics and science courses, as well as over discrimination in medical schools and other predominantly male institutions.

The impact of Title IX—and its opening of educational opportunities for females—is seen in all aspects of society. In the last fifteen years, an increasing number of women entered the work force. The Women's Bureau *1988 Fact Sheet on Women Workers* reported that women made up 44.8 percent of the labor force in 1987, with nearly equal labor force participation rates among black, latina, and white women. Women represented 38 percent of all executives, managers, and administrators in 1987 compared to 22 percent in 1975.

The number of women who earn degrees in business, engineering, and medicine is increasing each year. Specifically, there were over 100,000 female doctors in 1988, more than double the number in 1975, due in large part to Title IX's provision forbidding sex discrimination in admission to professional schools. The number of women scientists and engineers has more than tripled in the years between 1976 and 1986.

In sports, Title IX forced many colleges and universities to restructure completely their approach to women athletes by requiring that women receive scholarships, teams, coaches, and facilities equal to those of male athletes. The number of women in college athletics increased from 16,000 in 1972 to 150,000 in 1985. For instance, in 1989 the athletic budget for Texas women athletes was $3.5 million, as compared to $75,000 in 1975. And Title IX has meant that girls at the middle school and high school levels now have a much greater choice in individual and team sports than previously, and that athletics for girls is more visible within schools at the local and state levels.[5] However, it is important to note that the University of New Hampshire's women's basketball team—as the only undefeated basketball team, male or female, in the country—continues to receive little local or national notice.

But with these gains, major obstacles and inequities are still evident. As Deborah Rhode, director of the Institute for Research on Women and

Gender at Stanford points out, "Statutes have been enacted to secure similar treatment for persons similarly situated; less effort has been centered on remedying the structural factors that contribute to women's dissimilar and disadvantaged status."[6] And, although no educational institution has been penalized for noncompliance with Title IX, major inequities remain. But beyond the question of actual paper compliance remains the entire arena of social transformation. If Title IX, as we assume, was established to infuse gender-fair education into all aspects of our society, we must explore what lasting impact twenty years of Title IX has had. From this perspective, it may be that we are in fact in compliance with the letter of the law, but not the spirit.

The intent of Title IX was to provide equitable education for female students and equitable education opportunities for female teachers and administrators. While this vision has expanded over the years to incorporate issues of equity for both females and males, we as a nation still seem to be struggling with meeting the letter of the law, rather than moving to embrace the spirit of the vision. As one state administrator has said, "Title IX legislation has provided access to more programs for females and supports the philosophy that females now have unlimited opportunities to achieve excellence in school. Unfortunately, because of gender role socialization, females are not often exercising these options. Title IX has encouraged the system to be fair and open; the system, for the most part, has become more open and accessible. Yet little/nothing has changed."[7]

The twentieth anniversary of Title IX also coincided with a series of reports by the American Association of University Women (AAUW) that synthesized the bulk of research findings on the status of equitable education for females. The final report, *Shortchanging Girls* raised national awareness that—despite the existence of federal legislation that prohibits discrimination against women and girls in education—females remain at the margin of academic achievement. Yet, despite this overwhelming evidence, most schools continue to believe that they are in fact, educating all students equitably. Many believe that "since we've been in compliance with Title IX, it seems that gender does not play a role in the operation of our school system." Others feel that once addressed, the issue of gender equity is over and done with: "we attended a week workshop in the early 1970s and . . . I relayed the information from the workshop to our school personnel."

The question of compliance then may be explored from the lens of perception: How do schools perceive the issue of Title IX compliance? Do they see gender equity as a real issue within education? Is compliance with the law enough to achieve equity? Is it the impetus for social transformation, or do we need to move beyond the legal definition to a total systemic approach to equitable education for all students?

One state administrator reflecting on these questions said "[E]ducators take one of two positions in response to gender equity issues. Either they believe they already dealt with these issues way back in the 1970s after the regulations were first promulgated. Or they believe that of all the current and emerging issues facing educators—particularly issues of school reform/restructuring/improvement—equity is simply not as important."

She continued by linking Title IX compliance to the continued perpetuation of gender role stereotyping in our society:

> Until schools understand the process of gender role socialization, how dysfunctional it is and how schools contribute to gender role socialization, they will be unable to link the school experience with ultimate student outcomes. Compliance assures access in the school system but gender role socialization trains students to make traditional choices. As a result, being "fair" has produced few changes in student outcomes. Change will ultimately occur when systems are affirmative and challenge gender role socialization—which is not covered under Title IX. Title IX has contributed significantly to making education gender-fair. The issue, however, is not gender fairness in education, but how affirmative a school chooses to be in challenging the sex biases and sex-based expectations of its students, staff, parents, and community. Schools need to examine how their policies, practices, and the school climate are supporting two sets of expectations for students based on sex.

To discover the current perceptions of Title IX, we conducted a survey of equity specialists around the country, investigating both their perception of the overall impact of Title IX. We were interested in examining the vision of Title IX in relation to the reality of schools and wanted to see if those individuals charged with implementing Title IX felt that things had really changed in the last twenty years.

Are we educating students differently now, after two decades of Title IX, or do we continue to perpetuate gender-role stereotypes in our classrooms and in our education systems? National research continues to answer "no" and this answer is reinforced by the comments of sex-equity specialists across the country. As one state equity coordinator reminded us, "gender role socialization is 'alive and well' in schools. Students continue to be socialized in school to attach different meanings and value to gender."

RESEARCH BASE

While the AAUW report *Shortchanging Girls* precipitated national furor over the diminishing of females' involvement in education, the question has long been the focus of gender-equity specialists and organizations focused on gender equity. One such organization, the National Coalition for Sex Equity in Education (NCSEE) is the oldest national organization devoted to infusing gender fair education into schools and colleges. For fifteen years, the organization has provided support, training, and strategic assistance to gender-equity specialists working in state departments of education and higher education throughout the country. The individuals within the organization represent the range of expertise and experience found among those charged with institutionalizing Title IX within their localities. As a representative sample of gender-equity specialists, the NCSEE membership serves as a good indicator of the current impact of Title IX—both in terms of paper compliance and in terms of social transformation toward equity. It is to this organization that we first addressed our questions about the transformative impact of Title IX.

However, since the membership of NCSEE draws heavily from state-level experts, we wanted to compare their perceptions with those of equity coordinators working on the district or school-site level. Would the perceptions of local individuals, many of whom may have been appointed to the position or may have had little extended training in Title IX, be different from or supportive of the state-level coordinators? To do this, we asked each state to provide us with a list of its local Title IX people. Of the fifty states contacted, thirty-nine responded, and of those, twenty-seven states provided us with the names of local coordinators.

Together, our pool of potential respondents included approximately 300 NCSEE members and over 9,000 Title IX contacts. We then surveyed a random sampling of 2,000 Title IX contacts and all the NCSEE contacts. This enabled us to have a range of responses from most of the states and territories. A comprehensive survey was mailed to the 2,300 names, and follow-up phone interviews were scheduled with key respondents from each state. The responses were compiled and examined from two perspectives: first, we looked at the combined responses, particularly to the question of compliance, and then we examined the responses to determine any differences between the membership of NCSEE and those sex-equity coordinators who were not members of the organization.

IS COMPLIANCE ENOUGH?

As we conducted our research, we acknowledged our assumption that compliance was the beginning of a transformation process. However, our respondents reminded us that we might have been asking the wrong question. For example, a typical significant response from our respondents was, "Is compliance enough? We don't even have compliance." Or, as one respondent stated when asked if compliance was helping to transform her school, "I don't know. I've never seen full compliance."

The question of compliance became an indicator of philosophy toward gender equity. While most respondents (55 percent) felt that compliance was not enough to create the transformation of their schools into a gender-fair institution, a significant number (16 percent) felt that compliance with Title IX was enough. This points to a major philosophical split within gender equity that may, in fact, indicate a political split as well.

In the first group, respondents were primarily from urban and suburban centers, and were equally representational of males and females, administrators, teachers, and counselors. This group felt strongly that compliance was only a beginning—"but a precious beginning" according to one respondent. They were most concerned with attitudes and behaviors of students, teachers, and parents. This group saw Title IX as a way to begin a process, but also felt that systemic change needed to be constantly addressed. Additionally, they felt that the lack of federal support for regulating Title IX was hampering their work. The following responses indicate this group's feelings:

There is the "spirit" vs. the "letter" of the law issue. Staff development is a critical area and *old* habits die slowly. Unless pushed and prodded, some influential leaders do little beyond "letter" of the law to encourage positive change. (California)

I suppose progress has been made. But sometimes it seems like it's 100 years ago. Many educators don't know what we're talking about. Here's an example. Last year at the school I taught in, the second grade put on an assembly on careers, one for every letter of the alphabet. Twenty-one out of the twenty-six were stereotypes. The principal thought it was wonderful, had it taped and sent out to other schools. Maybe if sex equity were part of the curriculum, the children would point out these kinds of things to their teachers. (Massachusetts)

Discrimination covers only illegal, but not the bias and stereotyping behaviors that have long-term effects. Without staff preservice and inservice to eliminate unconscious bias we can't change. (New York)

Compliance relates to meeting requirements. Gender-fair is a concept requiring more than equality of things, materials, etc. Gender-fair requires a change in attitudes—sincere change. (Mississippi)

We need more than compliance. We need change in attitudes! We need more teacher inservice and more counseling inservice to create programs that are gender-free for all K-16 levels. (Illinois)

Our state has the attitude that OCR is not a threat so why change. The obvious is handled to some extent but overall we are a long way off. *Franklin v. Gwinnett* will help. (Idaho)

We have had Title IX, civil rights laws, employment laws, but discrimination is still practiced. Only when the laws are enforced and monitored will the laws be effective. Most institutions have paper compliance, but in reality they are not complying with the laws. (Texas)

Those in the combined group who felt compliance was sufficient were a much more heterogeneous group. For the most part they were from rural districts and schools (71 percent), were administrators, principals, or superintendents (86 percent), and were male (72 percent). Additionally, most indicated they were assigned to their work in gender equity, as opposed to the majority of respondents above who said they were drawn to equity work out of a sense of fairness. If this respondent group was disaggregated by NCSEE or non-NCSEE membership, we discovered that the majority of respondents in this group were not members of NCSEE. The non-NCSEE respondents were the most homogeneous group: 76 percent rural, 80 percent administrators, and 90 percent male. Many in this group felt they had already accomplished Title IX objectives as in "I think we're doing all we need to do." These respondents were concerned that there was too much emphasis placed on Title IX and equity. While they may have indicated that "yes" they felt compliance was enough, their responses were perfunctory, rather than expansive as in the above group. Some were concerned that too much attention was shown toward equity:

Being too aware and people dreaming up equity cases. Lawmakers have stirred up a can of worms and the[y] better be ready to deal with all the suits and *false* accusations.

Their responses indicated they felt the work was done or that compliance itself was not necessary. The implication of this for how they might enforce even the minimal compliance with Title IX is a matter of concern:

There is now an "accepted" attitude toward equal opportunities for both sexes, especially in students themselves. (Montana)

The only thing that remains separated and unequal is restroom times and rough body contact sports. (Indiana)

I have never had sex biases. I send teachers and administrators to multicultural conferences, have staff development (inservice) on multicultural education. (Mississippi)

In our part of the country, hiring in schools, except possibly for the superintendent, has to deal mostly with females against females. Females, not because of access or counseling, but because of marriage and child rearing, are not qualified in numbers. When they are—and apply—I see them being hired as top administrators. . . . I think enough has been spent, and that enough is being done. (Missouri)

Another significant difference between these two perspectives involved the impact of federal support for gender equity. When asked what would happen if federal financial support for gender equity stopped (e.g., WEEA, Carl Perkins), or if the government ceased to press for compliance with Title IX, a similar response emerged. The majority of respondents felt that gender-equity efforts would cease, would be significantly curtailed, and that most of their states, universities, or schools would not replace the funds.

The progress we have started to make would deteriorate rapidly. (Illinois)

Most funding would be gone. No training would be provided. The court and ultimately the legislature would arbitrate problems. (Utah)

Programs would be eliminated. Our districts have paper compliance and equity is not a priority. . . . Everything would basically be eliminated. Federal funds is the only thing driving some people to push. (Wisconsin)

All or most vocational programs for sex equity would end. Most technical assistance for Title IX would end. When OCR was ''enforcing'' there was improvement; since OCR no longer is perceived as doing their job, much of the improvement has disappeared. (Florida)

Those respondents who felt compliance was enough, however, felt that the elimination of federal funding or support for gender equity would have little effect on their work. Because they did not reflect a sense that gender equity was a process for social transformation, these respondents answered more narrowly.

> We use the state offices for workshops for teachers. (New Hampshire)

> We would continue as is since we require no funds and get no funds. (Indiana)

> Probably no changes at all because whatever is available would be shared. (Montana)

> None, as we have bought into and believe in those programs that exist here and would continue to do so. (but) . . . The district would replace little or no funds. (Missouri)

GROUP MEMBERSHIP AND PERCEPTIONS

To understand how gender-equity specialists across the country perceive the impact of Title IX, we asked respondents to answer a number of questions relating to Title IX understanding, leadership, institutionalization, compliance, and impact, all from the perspective of their institution. For instance, if the respondent were a teacher in a school building, they were to answer the question in terms of that building, or, if the respondents were state gender-equity coordinators, from the perspective of the state as a whole.

We also wanted to see if there was a relationship between perceptions of Title IX effectiveness and group membership, specifically in organizations such as NCSEE that focus on equity. Overall, the answers of NCSEE and non-NSCEE respondents showed differences in perceptions in every area we surveyed. NCSEE respondents, generally from urban, state-level institutions, and committed to gender equity enough to join a national organization, tended to rate their institutions lower than did their counterparts who were not members of NCSEE.

Group membership in an organization often implies an agreement with the vision and mission of the organization. Since its beginning the National Coalition for Sex Equity in Education has promulgated a vision of educational equity that includes gender and race, class, disability, sexual preference, and age. And while it remains beyond the scope of our research, we still must ask if members of NCSEE select the organization because it shares their vision of gender equity, or does membership in NCSEE help to change member attitudes? Our research showed that in many areas, membership or non-membership in NCSEE paralleled perceptions of the impact and reach of Title IX.

An important indicator of this difference in perception is highlighted by responses to the question "To what degree is your institution(s) in compliance with Title IX?" Based on a scale of 1 to 5, with one as "little/no" and 5 as "high," the average NCSEE response was 3.3, while the average non-NCSEE membership was 4.3 (Table 6.1).

Again, the question of membership vision surfaces in this examination. The question remains: does this difference in perception reflect the locus of work, or is it somehow connected more to membership in an organization that enables individuals fully to understand the complexity of the issue and trains them to be more reflective in their analysis of current impact.

Additionally, NCSEE respondents, as the mandated Title IX coordinators, can be assumed to be more aware than the average person about the intricacies of regulations and compliance with the regulations, and also about how their organization fits in with other schools, districts, or states in terms of compliance and social transformation. However, we must remember that these responses do not mean that the institutions NCSEE members work with have less understanding of the issues or are less in compliance than other institutions. Rather, for whatever reason, NCSEE

Table 6.1   *To what degree is your institution(s) in compliance with Title IX regulations?*

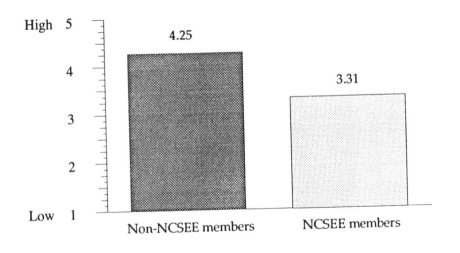

members perceive less institutional understanding, etc. than do non-NCSEE respondents. Some possible explanations of these different perceptions include NCSEE members' being more aware, and therefore more critical, of institutions, as well as their knowing more about national standards for sex equity and ways in which to measure equitable education.

Questions dealing with understanding sex-equity issues, institutionalization of regulations and goals, compliance, and impact of Title IX were used to compare responses from the two groups. NCSEE respondents gave an average rating of 2.35 to their institutions on the question "To what degree do you feel there is a general understanding of the sources of sex discrimination and bias specified in the Title IX regulations and their operation?" Non-NCSEE respondents gave an average rating of 3.04 (Table 6.2). The ratings stayed almost exactly the same when respondents rated institutional understanding of bias not specified in Title IX (Table 6.3). When questioned on the level of institutional understanding of the relationship between educational bias and sex differences in education and career outcomes, NCSEE respondents gave an average rating of 2.53, while non-member respondents rated their schools higher—3.24 (Table 6.4). The same pattern held in questions about institutionalization of Title IX requirements (Table 6.5) and knowledge of available models and resources (Table 6.6).

Table 6.2　　*To what degree do you feel there is a general understanding of the sources of sex discrimination and bias specified in Title IX regulations and their operation?*

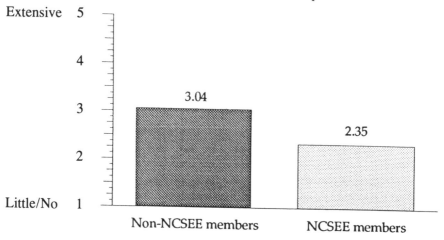

Table 6.3   *How much understanding is there of sources not addressed in the Title IX regulations (e.g., stereotyping in curriculum) and their operation?*

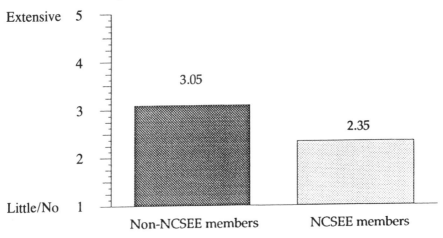

Table 6.4   *To what extent do you believe there is an understanding of the possible relationships between sex discrimination and stereotyping in education and sex differences in education and career outcomes?*

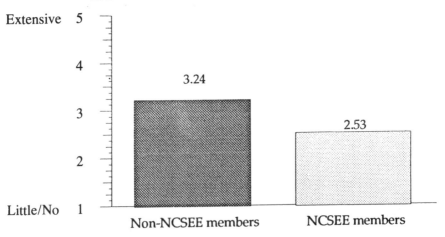

Table 6.5 *To what degree have the requirements of Title IX and the concerns related to sex equity in education been specified and incorporated into the policies, program plans, and management procedures of your educational institutions and agencies?*

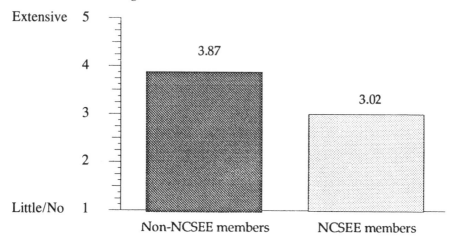

Table 6.6 *To what degree do models for such specification and incorporation exist?*

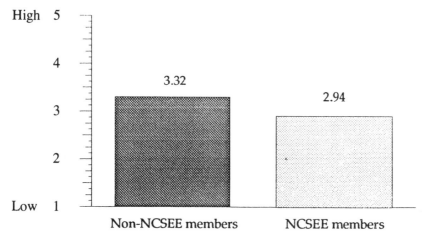

Interesting findings surfaced in responses to the questions asked regarding the impact of Title IX on the respondents' institutions. Respondents were asked to rate the impact of Title IX on the following areas: (1) impact on institution; (2) academic achievement for females; (3) access to nonacademic program and services for females; (4) faculty behavior toward students; (5) faculty attitudes about females; (6) student-teacher interactions; (7) student behaviors; (8) student attitudes toward sex-role stereotypes; (9) building coalitions with other equity movements; (10) white females; (11) females of color; (12) females with disabilities; and (13) males. While overall, NCSEE respondents rated impact lower than non-NCSEE respondents, the difference was not significant (Table 6.7). Both groups felt that impact was greatest in terms of overall impact on the institution, on females' access to nonacademic programs and services (with athletics specifically mentioned), and on white females. Both NCSEE members and nonmembers rated the impact on student behaviors and on males in the bottom third. This result seems to bear out a national perception that Title IX primarily benefits white females and that Title IX is primarily concerned with athletics. The disparity between this general-

Table 6.7
Non-NCSEE and NCSEE ratings of areas
of highest and lowest impact of Title IX.

	Non-NCSEE Members	**NCSEE Members**
Highest	1. Females' access to non-academic programs and services	1. Impact on institution
	2. Impact on institution	2. Females' access to non-academic programs and services
	3. Impact on white females	3. Impact on white females
	* * * * *	
	11. Impact on males	11. Impact on student behaviors
	12. Impact on student behaviors	12. Impact on males
Lowest	13. Impact on building coalitions with other equity movements	13. Impact on females with disabilities

ized perception and the reality needs to be fully documented and brought to both the public awareness and the consciousness of gender-equity specialists themselves.

An interesting difference in responses occurred in the rating of the extent to which Title IX had an impact on the ability to form coalitions with other groups. NCSEE respondents rated this as fourth highest, while nonmember respondents rated this thirteenth, the least affected of all the areas listed. Some of this variance can be attributed to the overall characteristics of both groups. The average NCSEE member is almost certainly more inclined to emphasize coalition building than the nonmembers. Whether this is because coalition builders are more likely to join an organization like NCSEE or because NCSEE membership provides more opportunities to build coalitions, or a combination of both, needs to be examined. However, it is also likely that district and school-based personnel who work in gender equity are more likely to be isolated from others and perhaps either do not see gender equity as an integral part of other equity movements, or do not have opportunities to interact with such groups.

INFLUENCE OF RESPONDENTS'
LOCATION AND ROLE

The difference in perception among these two groups becomes even more informative when we look at the breakdown of respondents by location and role. State-level personnel may have a total sense of the impact of Title IX across their states as opposed to those staff who work within a dis-

Table 6.8

Characteristics of Respondents
(Percent of responses)

	NCSEE	Non-NCSEE
Urban	63	16
Suburban	24	30
Rural	11	55
Work in state agency	18	62
Work in school district	18	62
Work in school building	11*	25**

*All of the NCSEE respondents were in secondary schools.
**60 percent of the non-NCSEE respondents worked in elementary schools.

trict or school and who may have a narrower sense of the overall impact of Title IX. Similarly, there seems to be a difference in perception between those who work in secondary schools and those in elementary schools. As one state-level respondent explained, "We find very few Title IX violations in elementary buildings. We find more violations at the secondary level." It may be that some of the compliance issues of gender equity do not surface until then, when the distinctions in such areas as athletics and physical education, sexual harassment, differential treatment, and class selection are more obvious.

A comparison of responses based on settings shows that NCSEE members rated their institutions lower overall, regardless of whether they worked in urban, suburban, or rural settings. Sex-equity coordinators who did not belong to NCSEE and who worked in rural and suburban settings rated their institutions' understanding, institutionalization of Title IX, and compliance with the regulations highest, while NCSEE urban and suburban respondents rated themselves lowest.

Table 6.9   *To what degree do you feel there is a general understanding of the sources of sex discrimination and bias specified in the Title IX regulations and their operation?*

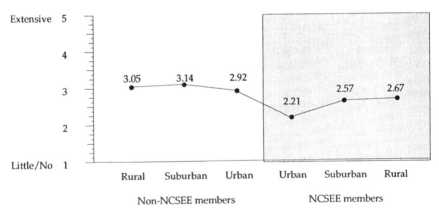

Table 6.10   *How much understanding is there of sources not addressed in the Title IX regulations (e.g., stereotyping in curriculum) and their operation?*

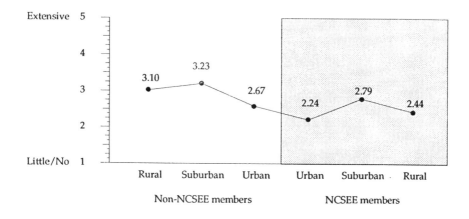

Table 6.11   *To what extent do you believe there is an understanding of the possible relationships between sex discrimination and stereotyping in education and sex differences in education and career outcomes?*

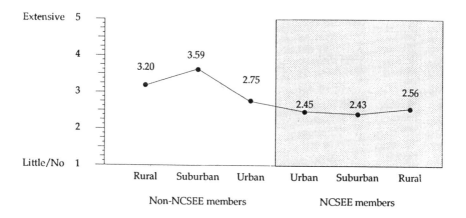

Table 6.12   *To what degree have the requirements of Title IX and the concerns related to sex equity in education been specified and incorporated into the policies, program plans, and management procedures of your educational institutions and agencies?*

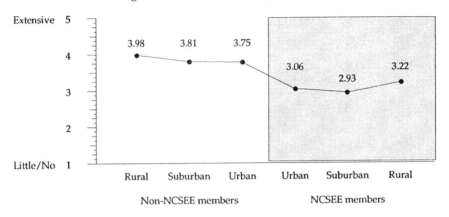

Table 6.13   *To what degree do models for such specification and incorporation exist?*

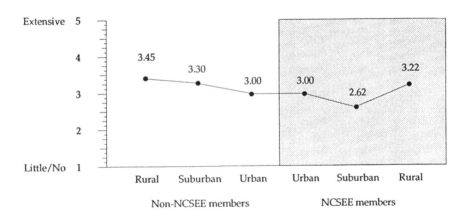

Table 6.14   *To what degree is your institution(s) in compliance with*
              Title IX regulations?

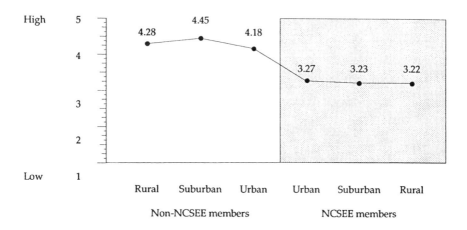

When asked to identify their place of work as either a state agency, school district, school building, junior or community college, or college or university, responses of both NCSEE members and nonmembers were closer in terms of perception of their institutions' understanding of Title IX. Overall, regardless of NCSEE membership, state agency respondents were in closer agreement in their ratings than were school district and school-building respondents from the two groups. One predominant pattern that emerged was that school-building personnel who were members of NCSEE tended to rate their institutions the lowest of the subgroups, while school-building personnel who were not members rated their schools the highest of all subgroups in every case.

This general agreement between NCSEE member and nonmember state agency responses did not extend to respondents' judgments of institutional knowledge of resources related to Title IX (where nonmember state agencies rated their institutions' knowledge lowest of all compared to the other subgroups and more than a whole point lower than NCSEE state agency personnel) and institutional compliance with Title IX regulations (where again non-NCSEE state agency respondents rated their state compliance lower than any other subgroup, and almost two points lower than the next lowest non-NCSEE subgroup).

Table 6.15   *To what degree do you feel there is a general understanding of the sources of sex discrimination and bias specified in the Title IX regulations and their operation?*

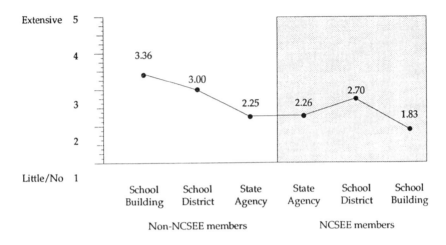

Table 6.16   *How much understanding is there of sources not addressed in the Title IX regulations (e.g., stereotyping in curriculum) and their operation?*

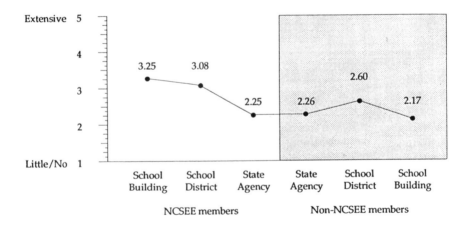

Table 6.17   *To what extent do you believe there is an understanding of the possible relationships between sex discrimination and stereotyping in education and sex differences in education and career outcomes?*

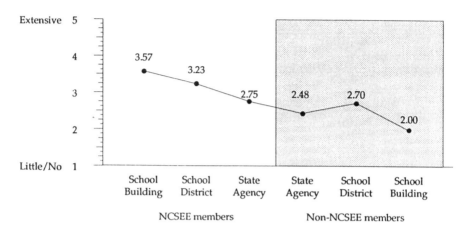

Table 6.18   *To what degree have the requirements of Title IX and the concerns related to sex equity in education been specified and incorporated into the policies, program plans, and management procedures of your educational institutions and agencies?*

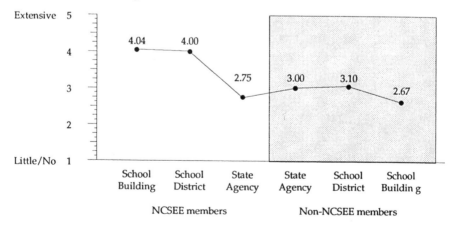

Table 6.19   *To what degree do models for such specification and incorporation exist?*

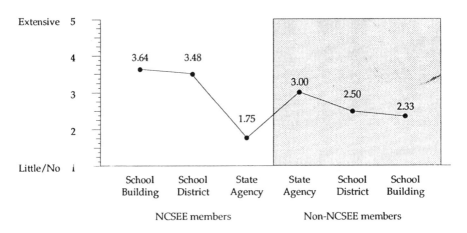

Table 6.20   *To what degree is your institution(s) in compliance with Title IX regulations?*

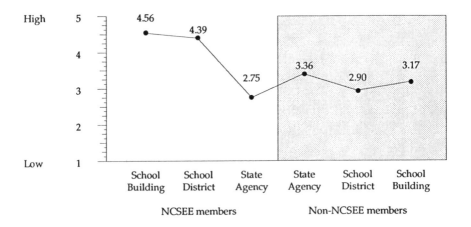

The amount of training or exposure to gender-equity concepts and to the mandates of Title IX seem to have a direct correlation to respondents' level of satisfaction with local compliance with the law. For instance, a large number of the state agency personnel had considerable training or experience in dealing with Title IX compliance issues. From this perspective, they were much more aware of the components of Title IX, its implications, and reporting requirements. They too had higher expectations for compliance than did many of the school-based Title IX coordinators. While school-based staff focused on Title IX issues that have received significant media coverage, such as sports (this was prior to the current interest in sexual harassment), they often did not have a sense that there were other equally valid concerns. Clearly, in order to be effective as a Title IX coordinator, staff must have a full understanding of the law, its implications, and an awareness of strategies for incorporating gender-fairness into all aspects of the school life. Such training is severely lacking for the majority of educators now charged with responsibility for Title IX. It should be noted that, ultimately, it is the chief school officer who is responsible for the implementation of Title IX, yet there seems to be little connection with the chiefs or little awareness on their part of the importance of Title IX both on the district and the state level. Even in those states with strong support from the state chief school officer, many respondents reported a lack of support or interest from local superintendents or principals.

In the late 1970s the WEEA contracted with the Council of Chief State School Officers to provide assistance to state education departments and local education institutions on Title IX implementation. This assistance was the few times that administrators have had the opportunity to become aware of gender-equity implications in education and receive training in approaches to equitable education. This intensive work helped coalesce a group of committed educational-equity specialists that have continued the work of gender equity to this day and who formed the core of the founders of the National Coalition for Sex Equity in Education. This important training, edited by Shirley McCune and Martha Matthews, is still a relevant and much needed model for continued education of equity professionals and education administrators.[8]

It also seems that distance may add to the different perceptions expressed by state and local gender-equity coordinators. State-level coordinators, in addition to their length of experience, tend to see their states in their entirety and have a fuller picture of how Title IX is addressed, and have a sense of how Title IX is administered in other states. School-or district-based staff may not have a basis for comparison and may see a school's efforts only in relation to what was done or not done in the past. Additionally, staff on the school level may feel somewhat hindered in efforts to implement gender-fair education within the school since this may not be an accepted social value among his or her colleagues. The pressure to conform, to ignore the issue, may in fact outweigh the desire to do something. The local norms and values must be addressed in any efforts to institute gender-fair education on the school level.

While school-based coordinators may be more aware of materials and may ask for resources to help, there does not seem to be much connection between the local schools and either the state department of education or the resources of the desegregation assistance centers, except in a few states. This may be an indicator of the very limited funds available to equity resources; each year the budgets for equity efforts are reduced making it difficult both to alert individuals to the existence of services and to provide intensive support and resources to schools. For instance, while the federal funds for the military escalate, and funds earmarked to science and mathematics education continue to grow, funds for race and sex equity remain at or below the same level as twenty years ago. Yet with minute amounts of money, gender-equity coordinators are charged with infusing gender-fair concepts into every classroom and school administration in the country. Without the support of the Office of Civil Rights and without financial support necessary to provide for a national restructuring of education, gender-equity specialists and Title IX coordinators still attempt to transform education into a system that is truly equitable for white females and students of color. They have not yet given up their efforts to attain even compliance, much less the vision that guided the creation of Title IX.

HOW DO WE GO BEYOND COMPLIANCE?

Despite the difference in perspectives among the four groups of respondents, when it came to the question of how to move beyond compliance, there was significant agreement among most respondents. Their responses could be grouped into several categories, three of which have significant implications for education: teacher training and staff development, family and community attitudes, policy, and the media representation of women. Many respondents indicated a need for "one hell of a lot of inservice" on the K-12 level as well as for "specific gender-fair training at the college level for entering teachers." As one of the more thoughtful respondents said,

> I really think that teacher preparation programs must be infused with gender-equity measurements. I am tired of doing "bandaid" training and inservice on generation after generation of teachers. Why are universities and colleges so enthusiastic about multicultural education and always neglect gender-equity elements in teacher education?! Perhaps it is because NCATE doesn't have any gender-specific criteria for accreditation of teaching colleges?

As she continued to talk, her comments on continuing the work over time should give us pause:

> Society's awareness at least of some areas of gender equity (sports and sexual harassment at this time) tend[s] to ebb and flow with media coverage. But the economic realities that our nation's profits will be endangered if more women and people of color are not fully trained and ready to work has really gotten people's attention. I desperately need more resources for my own program, and more resources designated with other's budgets to deal with systemic gender-equity change in an on-going way. (Montana)

Respondents see a clear connection between the role of education and the change in gender role expectations within the larger society.

> The K-12 school experience provides extensive preparation for students to interact with one another and to establish a set of values that extend to work, family, community and social roles. This preparation must include one set of expectations for all students regardless of gender. The ultimate outcomes this society is now witnessing (economic disparity, poverty, rage and violence, teen pregnancy) will continue until schools commit to examine (and changing) how they contribute to these outcomes through sex-biased expectations.

And the connections continue to an examination of how we develop and implement public policy.

> Legislative changes at the state and federal level should require that school improvement and school accreditation activity be grounded in assessments/self studies in which data on school outcomes are disaggregated by sex. Schools need to be convinced they have a "problem" with gender equity: hard data, documentation and self study can be used to confirm "problems" schools allege don't exist.

There exists a vast array of information and insight within the equity network that needs to be shared with policymakers as we move to the next step of implementation. At a time when we must still convince the nation that the education of women and girls is in the best interest of the country, we need to bring this information together and to develop a stronger sense of our collective vision of gender equity within a multicultural perspective. We need to begin to answer such questions as, "What is a gender fair pluralistic person, and how do they behave? What would gender fair accreditation standards look like? What is a national unified approach to gender-fair multicultural education? How do we raise the level of investment in gender-fair multicultural education, and how do we take what we know and apply it more broadly?''

If, after twenty years, we are still attempting to make systemic change happen without the funding and support to make that happen, we must examine not our national commitment to gender equity, but our strategy for making it happen. When the message from the leadership in business and government implies that education should do what the defense industry or the biotechnology industry have done by combining the best of business and education we can agree. But we cannot stop there, for unlike those examples of a winning combination, education for women and girls has not had the billions of dollars of investment. And, while money is not everything, it may be, as philosopher May West once said, ''the only thing'' that may help to support the ongoing infusion of the principles of Title IX into all aspects of education.

EDUCATIONAL EQUITY LEGISLATION
AND THE FUTURE

In reviewing the impact of Title IX legislation, we found it clear that the law has been an important beginning and has provided a valuable foundation in working to make educational systems more responsive to the needs of females. As a group of educational researchers concluded, ''Strong sex equity laws and/or policies can be considered a first step in achieving sex equity.''[9] Because of the massive systemic inequities in educational systems prior to Title IX, federal law has had significant impact. And where systems have not changed, students, educators, and others have legal recourse for dealing with discrimination.

Title IX has been able to influence systems and affect behaviors somewhat. The question of attitudes and of meeting the spirit of the law has been more difficult. This was especially evident during the second decade of the legislation, when there was little federal support or leadership for states and localities. Many equity advocates interviewed reflect the feeling that as a result of the mixed messages from Congress and the courts during the 1980s, the lack of enforcement, and the increased challenges from the administration during this period, gender equity has actually lost ground.

As the U.S. enters its third decade under Title IX, it is clear that there is still much work to do in encouraging and helping educational institutions to eliminate discriminatory practices and policies. Title IX can provide strong support for these efforts, especially given the Supreme Court's most recent interpretation. The work of Title IX can be strengthened through additional legislative and policy efforts. As Sundra Flansburg has suggested in "Legislation for Change,"[9] several key components need to be addressed, including:[10]

1. Legislation needs strong governmental leadership and a commitment to monitoring compliance.
2. Legislation needs strong grassroots support and action to work. Social change cannot be dictated solely from above. In the case of Title IX, support and action for community based groups and local schools are vital for effectively translating goals and vision into concrete action.
3. Strong links between local action, policymakers and monitoring institutions are vital. In order to maintain living legislation that is addressing real needs, policymakers and administrators must be connected to people who are working in the field in order to share current issues and concerns from the local level.
4. Legislation should be sufficiently broad to deal with new issues arising in equity.
5. To be effective, legislation should include a requirement for early evaluation and plans for compliance. This action pushes the institutions to consider the implications of gender equity early on and encourages them to develop short- and long-term plans for remedying inequities. Such planning and evaluation also provides important data for analyzing the effectiveness of the legislation.
6. Specific and strong consequences for noncompliance—that are actually carried out. Until the *Franklin v. Gwinnett* ruling, no educational institution had lost federal funds for noncompliance with Title IX. The possibility of having to pay monetary damages from a suit may encourage compliance in a way the monitoring process has not to date.
7. Set up supporting efforts that provide incentives and assistance to institutions and systems. A key element of the success of Title IX has been the assistance provided to institutions to identify issues and evaluate compliance, as well as the provision of training and materials to assist institutions to make changes. This includes the services and resources of such federally funded projects as the Desegregation Assistance Centers (which provide services to schools within each federal region on race, sex, and linguistic desegregation) and the WEEA Publishing Center (which provides consultation, resources, and materials to schools to help with gender fair education).
8. Provide for documentation and dissemination of model programs, training, and materials.

9. Give assistance to institutionalize exemplary programs. As Klein has suggested, funding and assistance to arrange peer review and field testing of promising programs, and then assistance in adapting them to different locations, forms the first step toward widespread institutionalization of equitable education models.

10. Strengthen a strong national infrastructure dedicated to equity work. This includes linking the Desegregation Assistance Centers, the WEEA projects, the WEEA Publishing Center, along with such organizations as NCSEE, the National Coalition of Women and Girls in Education, the Project on Equal Education Rights (NOW Legal Defense and Education Fund), and teacher and research organizations such as the National Education Association, American Federation of Teachers, and the American Educational Research Association in a system of research and practice that both develops and promotes gender-fair multicultural education.

REFERENCES

Katherine Hanson is the director of the Women's Educational Equity Act (WEEA) Publishing Center and Associate Director for the Center for Equity and Cultural Diversity at EDC. The work here was supported solely by the Center for Equity and reflect her personal views. This study and report were prepared with the help of Sundra Flansburg in her role as colleague in the Center for Equity. It was presented at the annual meeting of the American Educational Research Association, San Francisco, California, April 1992.

NOTES

1. P. Cheng, "State Title IX Laws." Ph.D diss., 1986.
2. Nancy Vargas and the National Women's Law Center are currently developing a full analysis of the recent *Franklin v. Gwinnett* court case, its implications and ramifications for gender equity.
3. For a fuller discussion of sexual harassment see the works of N. Stein, E. Linn, and S. Klein. For a discussion of the implications of Title IX, sexual harassment and *Franklin v. Gwinnett,* see N. D. Stein, 1993, "It happens here, too: Sexual Harassment and Child Sexual Abuse in Elementary and Secondary Schools." In *Gender and Education,* S. K. Biklen and D. Pollard eds. (Chicago: University of Chicago Press).
4. M. Dunkle, 1989, *Just what the doctor should have ordered: A prescription for sex-fair school health services* (Newton, MA.: WEEA Publishing Center, Education Development Center).

5. K. Hanson, and S. Flansburg, 1989, *Empowerment education: An examination of WEEA and its projects* (Newton, MA: Education Development Center).
6. D. L. Rhode, 1990, Gender equality and employment policy, in *The American woman, 1990–91: A status report,* ed. S. E. Rix (New York: W. W. Norton), 174.
7. This and all the following unreferenced quotes are from conversations and from questionnaires about Title IX that I administered in 1991–92.
8. The training package, *Implementing Title IX and attaining sex equity: A workshop package,* was available from the Superintendent of Documents, U.S. Government Printing Office.
9. P. A. Schmuck, et al., 1985, Administrative strategies for institutionalizing sex equity in education and the role of government, in *Handbook for achieving sex equity in education,* ed. S. S. Klein (Baltimore: Johns Hopkins University Press).
10. S. Flansburg, and K. Hanson, 1993, Legislation for change: A case study of Title IX and the women's educational equity act program. A paper presented at the Fifth International Interdisciplinary Congress on Women, San José, Costa Rica.

REGULATORY COMPLIANCE
AND THE CULTURE OF THE SCHOOLS:
THE CASE OF SPECIAL EDUCATION

Kathleen Kelley Lynch and
Steven S. Goldberg

THE PROBLEM

When Congress passed the Education for All Handicapped Children Act of 1975 ("EAHCA" or "PL 94–142"), it initiated a chain of events that has had profound consequences for education. Some consequences, such as increased funding, were intended, while others, such as increased conflict, were not. The changes precipitated by EAHCA have been characterized by two currents. The first is legal: because courts are responsible for interpreting disputed questions of law, special education statutes have gained their meaning primarily through litigation of actual fact situations. The second current is structural: to comply with policy mandates, schools have had to adopt changes in their modus operandi that have modified the roles, rules, and relationships that characterize public schools.

This chapter follows the course of the litigation and restructuring precipitated by EAHCA and analyzes the consequences of change created by the meeting of these two currents. It examines the role of law over the last two decades in modifying the structure and culture of the schools, and on the capacity of schools to accommodate handicapped students. A fundamental premise of this chapter is that the EAHCA (renamed the Individuals with Disabilities Education Act or "IDEA" in 1990) imposed changes on the schools that are incompatible with their culture because the law was conceptualized in a legal, rather than education framework. We examine the idea that the very safeguards and rights provided by EAHCA have impeded its implementation. A critical question is whether the changes resulting from EAHCA have fundamentally restructured the schools to assimilate values incorporated in the law, or whether the changes are superficial; if so, following the law may give the appearance of compliance, while protecting the same school culture that generated the need for legal mandates in the first place. Has EAHCA been an "effective instrument of social reform" (Singer & Butler, 1987), or "the principal barrier to achieving the spirit of the law" (Skrtic, 1990)? Finally, we suggest strategies for fulfilling the intent of the law by restructuring schools to remove artificial barriers between regular education and special education.

RESTRUCTURING AND EDUCATION

Definitions of Restructuring

Restructuring has been the major focus of educational scholars and practitioners over the past several years. In spite of the intense interest in this field, there is no single common definition contained in the research and numerous reports. Nevertheless, the school restructuring literature highlights a number of recurrent themes. Included in the varied notions of restructuring are a decentralization of decision making and a focus at the school-building level; the mandate to educate all students; an emphasis on raising and clarifying results; the involvement of parents and other education stakeholders; and, altered roles and responsibilities for education personnel. Basom and Crandall (1989) write of realigning roles, relationships and responsibilities in order to offer new and different options to students. A common theme is that restructuring is a fundamental redesign, not just change for the sake of change. Sarason (1990) maintains that reform and restructuring require that we discard the old assumptions on which the current system is built, and also change the power relationships that inhibit positive change. Elmore (1990) concurs, asserting that effective restructuring should balance power and influence among school constituencies: parents, administrators, students, and teachers.

Corbett articulates a concise but complete definition, which incorporates the main goals of restructuring, and which we therefore adopt for the purposes of this discussion: "A social system's structure is its pattern of rules, roles, and relationships. Restructuring, then, represents a change in these social characteristics. However restructuring is not simply for restructuring's sake; its sole purpose is to produce substantially different results from those a district is currently producing. Thus, restructuring involves alterations in a school district's pattern of rules, roles, relationships, and results."

The pattern of a school district's rules, roles, relationships, and results defines such variables as the instructional technology, the role and status of teachers, and the relationship of parents to the school and educational process. These variables directly affect the restructuring process.

Working with these factors and with the various definitions of restructuring, Elmore (1990) has synthesized some common themes, which he organized around three distinct approaches. The first approach emphasized reforming the core technology of schools, that is, the content of schooling and the methods employed to deliver that content. Elmore's second approach focused on reforming the occupational conditions of teaching. The third focused on reforming the relationship between schools and their consumers.

The Restructuring Movement, Special Education, and the Dual System

Discussions about special education have been remarkably absent from the research and rhetoric about restructuring public education (Hornbeck, 1992). None of the drafters of major reform reports incorporated special education into their vision of a new education system; it is simply absent from the reports, or addressed only superficially (Pugach & Sapon-Shevin, 1987). Sarason (1990) believes that the current generation of reformers accepts the system the way it is. He charges that "reformers rivet on problems they can deal with and gloss over problems they often regard as more important, but too controversial." (1990, p. 29).

Special education developed as a response to the failure of regular education (Skrtic, 1990; Gartner & Lipsky, 1987; Reynolds, et al., 1987). Students whose needs do not fit within the margins of traditional school services are squeezed out of the system into one that can more closely meet their needs (Skrtic, 1990). Hornbeck (1992), moreover, asserts that the reason most children are referred to special education is because regular education cannot provide them with the support and services they need. Several assumptions underlie the perceived need for a separate system of education for some students. First, it assumes that there are two distinct categories of student: those whose needs can be met within the system, and those whose needs cannot be met ("normal" and "handicapped" students). Second, it assumes that regular education does not possess the appropriate educational technology to address students who are not "normal." Third, it assumes that "special" educators possess specialized skills and knowledge to meet the needs of "handicapped" students and that "regular" educators do not have the appropriate resources (Gartner & Lipsky, 1987; Reynolds, et al., 1987).

Culture and Change in the Schools

Central to the problem of change is the notion of organizational culture (Sarason, 1990, 1982; Skrtic, 1990). Culture has been defined as (1) a pattern of basic assumptions, (2) invented, discovered, or developed by a given group, (3) as it learns to cope with its problems of external adaptation and internal integration, (4) that has worked well enough to be considered valid and, therefore is (5) to be taught to new members as the (6) correct way to perceive, think and feel in relation to these problems. Culture manifests itself through its values and underlying assumptions. These assumptions are based on "traumatic" experiences in the organization's history (such as lawsuits) and lead members of the organization to resist similar experiences. This is the reason that culture is difficult to change (Schein, 1990).

Fullen describes how the culture of the schools is resistant to accommodation and change: "like almost all other complex traditional social organizations, the schools will accommodate in ways that require little or no change. This is not to say that the accommodation is insincere or deliberately cosmetic, but rather that the strength of the status quo—its underlying axioms, its pattern of power relationships, its sense of tradition and therefore what seems right, natural and proper—almost automatically rules out options for change in the status quo."

People who are trying to change an organization by legal means must be aware that mandates imposed by external sources—such as litigation—have been and are strongly resisted by the essentially conservative culture of the schools. Although change may not occur in an organization without some external impetus (Fullan, 1991), Sarason believes that in the case of special education, the response of the public schools to EAHCA is a *forced* accommodation to a perceived threat.

Skrtic has analyzed how the conservative culture of the school bureaucracy has failed to mesh with the cultural values on which EAHCA is based. He describes the public school as a professional bureaucracy—a place in which workers are specialized and the clients are distributed among a variety of workers who must provide complete services for clients. In a professional bureaucracy, this coordination is achieved through standardization of the workers' skills, which is itself honed through socialization in professional schools. Because of the intensive socialization provided to workers during their training, there is a convergence of thought and, consequently, a lack of adaptability. If a client's needs fall outside of the professional worker's skills, the client is either squeezed into an existing program of services, or sent to another professional who has a more appropriate set of skills or programs to offer. This professional bureaucracy operates, according to Skrtic, within an outer shell of machine bureaucracy. In the machine bureaucracy, the work is simple, and standardization is achieved through the routinization of a task. Like the professional bureaucracy, the machine bureaucracy is not an adaptable system. However, as Skrtic notes, the school, as a public organization, must respond to demands from the public for change. One way that it responds is by creating with symbols and ceremonies the illusion of change, while the organization remains essentially unchanged.

EAHCA springs from a very different organizational structure, the adhocracy. While the bureaucracy is based on standardization, specialization, and inflexibility, the adhocracy is based on collaboration, mutual adjustment, and problem solving. According to Skrtic, "from one organizational perspective, the basic problem with the EHA [the Education of the Handicapped Act] is that it attempts to force an adhocratic value orientation on a professional bureaucracy as if it were a machine bureaucracy" (p. 172).

The intended result of the adhocratic EAHCA was to decrease the effects of student disability by customizing instruction in regular education settings. However, the bureaucratic culture and values of the schools, combined with the procedural requirements of the law, actually increased the number of students identified as handicapped and has exacerbated the inflexibility of both regular and special education classrooms. As a result, special education has become an island within regular education; on this island, diversity is accommodated and the rules of the traditional school structure do not apply; special education has its own rules. The procedural safeguards that were put into place to ensure that the diverse needs of handicapped students would be met within the regular education framework formed a barrier between special education and regular education. Thus, the letter of the law is followed, but the fundamental structure of the education establishment is safe. A dual system of education was institutionalized.

The dual system is plagued by what Reynolds, et al. call "the dual problems of disjointedness and proceduralism". Disjointedness refers to the phenomenon of launching a series of narrowly defined programs, each intended to meet very specific needs in an unconnected way. For example, one child may be assigned to a regular second-grade classroom, but attend a resource room one hour per day for reading help, see a speech therapist for several hours a week, or see an occupational therapist twice a week. Each service is delivered in a different place at a different time by a different professional. Each is trained according to a specialized body of knowledge that reflects differing values. Each provides a separate and distinct array of services. The four services (regular education, special education, speech therapy, occupational therapy) are brought together only on paper through an individualized education plan.

This disjointedness leads to proceduralism in two ways: First each narrowly defined program or service has its own eligibility criteria, categories or labels, and even its own funding mechanism (Reynolds, et al., 1987). Gaining entry into a program or obtaining a service requires that students undergo certain test procedures and meet certain criteria. Second, the law prescribes the process a student must undergo in order to be identified as handicapped and provided with services. This process is designed to ensure that legal rights have been protected and legal requirements met. Adherence to proper procedures keeps the courts and regulators at bay and ensures a smooth flow of government funds for local districts. Thus, school districts concentrate on following procedures as a way to avoid costly litigation, while at the same time maintaining their funding. An emphasis on proceduralism allows school officials to be meticulous in following the law without asking whether or not effective education is being provided (Hornbeck, 1992b). For this reason, legal requirements may undermine substantive change. How did this situation come about?

LITIGATION AND RESTRUCTURING

During the early 1970s, landmark lawsuits led Congress to pass EAHCA (Goldberg, 1982; Rothstein, 1989). Described as the major piece of social legislation passed during the last two decades (Pittenger & Kuriloff, 1982), its procedural requirements are well known. The statute requires states to provide formal due process hearings to parents who object to the educational classification, program, or placement school officials offer their children. The hearings include all of the elements generally thought to be essential to achieving individual justice. Participants have the right to receive adequate written notice, to examine school records, to legal representation, to call and examine witnesses, to have their case judged by an impartial hearing officer, and to appeal adverse decisions to state or federal court (Pub L. 94–142, 1990; CFR, 1991).

Congress imposed these procedures because it believed that they would secure parental participation in decision making, vital to their child's education. Most members of Congress—perhaps because they are lawyers—chose this legal approach because they believed that such procedures were the best way to achieve fairness and individual rights (Goldberg & Kuriloff, 1991; Kuriloff, 1985). The law has been the basis for an impressive array of litigation involving a panoply of issues for students who are thought to have mental or physical handicaps. Its advocates claim that the law has developed and defined the rights of so-called disabled students to an unprecedented degree (Singer & Butler, 1987). Moreover, proponents believe that the law has opened school policy to parental scrutiny and parent-initiated change. Its critics have found PL 94–142, along with related legislation, Section 504 of the Rehabilitation Act (1975), to be unworkable because it mandates expensive and unusual programs, has created an adversarial atmosphere in which to develop education programs, and its requirements undermine reform (Goldberg & Kuriloff, 1991; Skrtic, 1991; Gartner & Lipsky, 1987; Neal & Kirp, 1985).

The type of adversarial rights-based approach embodied in PL 94–142 is anathema to effective school restructuring. Reform requires decentralization of demands and independence on the part of individual schools; a clear district-wide reform effort, rather than uncoordinated projects forced piecemeal on local schools; an atmosphere where variety is emphasized over uniformity; accountability where local decision makers can act without dominance by legislatures; and schools where parental choice drives accountability in the local schools (Hill & Bonan, 1991). Legal rules are developed in a culture different from that of education and conflict with the elements required for school change (Goldberg & Lynch, 1992; Goldberg, 1989). For example, law is based on the reality that legal rights are enforced on a piecemeal basis through individual complaints and legislation that responds to advocacy pressure; it requires a centralized authority for enforcement; accountability is not to individuals but to authorities; and, decision making in response to law is in the negative—that is, school officials refuse to act based on a fear of litigation. In essence, law is imposed by outside forces on an unwilling local population—the worst possible way of doing business when restructuring is undertaken (Hill & Bonan, 1991; Hill & Madey, 1982).

There is a developing line of analysis that underscores the conflict between increased legalization of education, spurred by the rights approach, and the culture of the school, which needs a communitarian climate in order for work to be done (Handler, 1990, 1986). On the one hand, Yudof and Herr have written that the rights approach may be positive because school policies may be more fair to parents and students who in the past had no ability to participate in decisions made about them. Yet, the imposition of impersonal legal rules in an area where issues had been informally resolved leads to mistrust and conflict. Indeed, as Handler has suggested, an adversarial legal approach—especially in special education—has no place in an area where decisions must be continuous and discretionary, continuous in order to build relationships and discretionary because each child who needs help must receive unique treatment, not the formulaic individualized education programs PL 94-142 mandates.

Under PL 94-142, children must be said to fit special labels in order to receive funding for programs. Yet, applying the law here exacerbates inequality by seeking and maintaining difference; moreover, compliance requires already alienated administrators and parents to identify themselves to higher authorities as victims—people who are helpless and malfunctioning, rather than as individuals who are entitled to services and the funding to run them as they see fit (Minow, 1990; Bumiller, 1988). In fulfilling these highly prescriptive requirements, local administrators fall into a bureaucratic mode, creating subsystems to control parents and their children who need help. Indeed, the level of knowledge about special education programs is so primitive (Shaywitz et. al, 1992), that the ability to make discretionary school-based decisions (rather than engaging in mere procedural compliance) about individual children, which is consistent with effective reform, seems especially critical. Indeed, as a consequence of his observations of procedural compliance in special education, Handler (1986) emphasized that an effective special education decision-making process is one that is controlled by local administrators and parents working together.

The literature focusing on policy implementation describes the consequences that occur when external authorities impose legal procedures on local school officials, as well as on the parents and students who must comply with the rules they did not develop (Weatherly & Lipsky, 1978). This line of scholarship has identified a central obstacle to implementing proposed legal change: school administrators enforce laws in a number of ways that undermine legislative intent and judicial remedies (Goldberg, 1986). School politics and resistence, as well as the reality of the organizational structure of the school, often intervene to change law at the implementation site. For example, the pioneering RAND (Berman & McLaughlin, 1978) studies assert that federally imposed policy is not the way to accomplish local change; instead local school districts are the places where change could more effectively be initiated and implemented. Local participants must want to accomplish change because it cannot be imposed in an authoritarian way—from the "top-down." Local administrators must be brought into the process and trained; local expertise and technical assistance should guide project implementation; there must be frequent staff meetings and locally designed project materials; and there must be a pool of voluntary, highly motivated participants. Additionally, the implementation process must be one of "mutual adaptation"—the program and participants interact in a way that meets the purpose of the program, as well as local needs.

These earlier RAND findings include the elements and attitudes necessary for restructuring. (Hill & Bonan, 1991). School change efforts, as Handler's work suggests, are effective when parents and school administrators build relationships at the local level over a period of time because they live in a culture where outside pressure is resented and ignored (Sarason, 1990, 1982). It makes sense, then, that the literature of restructuring reinforces the concept of "bottom-up" change. In addition, very recent research about organizational behavior supports findings in education. For example, a Harvard Business School project that examined several large companies suggests that change can only be accomplished when people who work far removed from the top of a hierarchy begin to implement new projects (Beer, Eisenstat & Spector, 1990). Perhaps researchers of service organizations are beginning to understand that people who work in or are affected by the organization seek a culture that is supportive of their freedom to work and create and that emphasizes trust and support (Kotter & Heskett, 1992; Kanter, 1990); in essence, people understand that cooperating in the place that most immediately affects them is the most effective path to positive restructuring (Goleman, Kaufman & Ray, 1992; Sizer, 1992).

EDUCATIONAL REMEDIES

The literature on special education and school restructuring suggests several educational actions that policymakers and educators can take to remedy the dysfunctional situation that has resulted when law is imposed on educational policy. These actions aim at achieving a balance between legal concerns and educational concerns, at replacing the dual system of education with a single system, and at achieving a restructuring of schools that will benefit handicapped and non-handicapped children as well.

The first strategy focuses on outcome-based education, which would require a shift away from an emphasis on proceduralism to an emphasis on the educational substance of a student's program. It would also ascertain whether or not the substance of the program will result in the student's learning essential skills. Hornbeck (1992a, 1992b) points out that this approach is based on the school's embracing two assumptions: first, that all children can learn, and second, that the schools really do have more knowledge about how children learn and the tools to enhance that knowledge than they currently use. Outcome-based education requires that educators relinquish the notion of two types of students—handicapped and normal—and consider students as moving individually on a single skills continuum (Shaywitz, et al., 1992). It also requires that individual student needs be provided for within a unitary system (Hornbeck, 1992a, 1992b; Reynolds, et al., 1987; Gartner & Lipsky, 1987). For outcome-based education to work, schools are going to have to accommodate individual differences with flexibility and problem-solving, rather than with labeling and proceduralism.

A second strategy is the suspension of excessive procedures (Hornbeck, 1992a, 1992b; Reynolds, et al., 1987). Although legally prescribed procedures were initiated to protect the rights of handicapped children, we have described how procedures such as due process have been emphasized at the expense of educational substance. Although responsible educators advise against precipitously removing procedural safeguards, (Hornbeck, 1992a, 1992b; Reynolds, et al., 1987; Gartner & Lipsky, 1987), they do recommend a variety of experimental strategies that can be implemented alongside procedural protections. Hornbeck (1992a, 1992b) describes "schools of distinction," which would be restructured to allow students to achieve within a unitary system and without procedural requirements. Reynolds, et al. (1987) describe a similar approach in which a "waiver for performance" provides flexible interpretation of rules for selected schools that provide data on student outcomes. Under either system, schools would not be denied funding for adopting a non-labeling approach, nor would they be relieved of the responsibility to address students' rights to a free and appropriate education. These approaches endorse the notion of "rights without labels" (Reynolds, et al., 1987).

The implementation of outcome-based education and the suspension of onerous proceduralism are rather radical ideas for school officials entrenched in a bureaucratic modus operandi. As with any change, successful introduction of a new policy will require considerable staff training for teachers, administrators, and parents (Fullan, 1991). During the period of experimentation that Hornbeck (1992a, 1992b) and Reynolds, et al. (1987) describe, a process will be needed to resolve conflict and ease the integration of new practices into a newly restructured and more humane school organization.

Another strategy would reexamine the way law is used in education. From its outset, special education legal policy, through funding mechanisms and regulation, has rewarded disjointedness and proceduralism (Reynolds, et al., 1987). For restructuring to be successful, policymakers need to reframe their efforts so that school officials are rewarded for initiatives that meet the educational needs of students, while preserving their right to education. At the same time, courts need to recognize that parent-school relationships are not well served by litigation. Implementing alternatives to lawsuits, including meditation, would be useful in creating a trusting school climate necessary for effective reform (Goldberg & Lynch, in press; Goldberg & Kuriloff, 1991).

REFERENCES

Basom, R., and D. Crandall. 1989. Implementing a redesign strategy: Lessons from educational change. *Educational Horizons,* 69, (2), 73–77.

Beer, M., R. Eisenstat, and B. Spector. 1990. The critical path to corporate renewal. Boston: Harvard Business School Press.

Berman, P., and W. McLaughlin. 1978. Federal programs supporting educational change, vol VIII: *Implementing and sustaining innovations.* Santa Monica, CA: Rand Corporation.

Bumiller, K. 1988. *The civil rights society.* Baltimore: Johns Hopkins University Press.

Code of Federal Regulations.

Corbett, H. 1990. *On restructuring.* Philadelphia: Research For Better Schools.

Elmore, R. 1990. *Restructuring schools.* San Francisco: Jossey Bass.

Fullen, M. G. 1991. *The new meaning of educational change.* New York: Teachers College.

Gartner, A., and D. Lipsky. 1987. Beyond special education: Toward a quality system for all students. *Harvard educational review* 57:367–95.

Goldberg, S. 1986. Implementing legal change in the schools: Recent research and comments. *Planning and changing,* 17:209–15.

————. 1982. *Special education law: A guide for parents, advocates, and educators.* New York: Plenum.

Goldberg, S., and P. Kuriloff. 1991. Evaluating the fairness of special education hearings. *Exceptional children* 57:546–55.

Goldberg, S., and K. Lynch in press. Reconsidering the legalization of school reform: A case for implementing change through mediation. *Ohio State journal on dispute resolution.*

Goleman, D., P. Kaufman, and M. Ray. 1992. *The creative spirit.* New York: Dutton.

Handler, J. F. 1990. *Law and the search for community.* Philadelphia: University of Pennsylvania Press.

————. 1986. *The conditions of discretion: Anatomy, Community, Bureaucracy.* New York: Russell Sage.

Harvey, G., and D. Crandall. 1988. *A beginning look at the how and what of restructuring.* Andover, MA: Regional Laboratory For Educational Improvement.

Herr, S. 1983. *Rights and advocacy for retarded people.* Lexington, MA: Lexington Books.

Hill, P., and J. Bonan. 1991. *Decentralization and accountability in public education.* Santa Monica, CA: Rand.

Hill, P., and D. Madey. 1982. *Educational policymaking through the civil justice system.* Santa Monica, CA: Rand.

Hornbeck, D. 1992a. On the changing face of special education. *The new school administrator* 2:14–18.

Hornbeck, D. 1992b. *On the changing face of special education* (audiotape).

Kanter, R. 1989. The new managerial work. *Harvard Business Review* Nov.–Dec. 85–92.

Kotter, J. P., and J. Heskett. 1992. *Corporate culture and performance.* New York: Free Press.

Kuriloff, P. 1985. Is justice served by due process?: Affecting the outcome of special education hearings in Pennsylvania. *Law and contemporary problems* 48:89–118.

Minow, M. 1990. *Making all the difference: Inclusion, exclusion, and American law.* Ithaca: Cornell University Press.

Neal, D., and D. Kirp. 1985. The allure of legalization reconsidered: The case of special education. *Law and contemporary problems,* 48:63–87.

Pittenger, J., and P. Kuriloff. 1982. Educating the handicapped: Reforming a radical law. *The public interest* 66:72–96.

Reynolds, M., M. Wang, and H. Walberg. 1987. The necessary restructuring of special and regular education. *Exceptional children* 53:391–98.

Rothstein, L. 1989. *Special education law.* White Plains, NY: Longmans.

Sarason, S. B. 1990. *The predictable failure of educational reform: Can we change course before it's too late?* San Francisco: Jossey-Bass.

Sarason, S. 1982. *The culture of schools and the problem of change,* 2d ed. Needham Heights, MA: Allyn & Bacon.

Schein, E. 1990. Organizational culture. *American psychologist,* 45:109–119.

Shaywitz, S., M. Escobar, B. Shaywitz, J. Fletcher, and R. Makuch. 1992. Evidence that dyslexia may represent the lower tail of a normal distribution of reading ability. *The New England journal of medicine,* 325:145–50.

Singer, J., and J. Butler. 1987. The Education for All Handicapped Children Act: Schools as agents for social reform. *Harvard educational review* 57:125–52.

Sizer, T. 1992. *Horace's school: Redesigning the American High School.* Boston: Houghton Mifflin.

Skrtic, T. 1991. The special education paradox: Equity as the way to excellence. *Harvard educational review* 61:148–206.

Stainback, W., and S. Stainback. 1984. A rationale for the merger of special and regular education. *Exceptional children,* 51:102–11.

Weatherly, R., and M. Lipsky. 1977. Street level bureaucrats and institutional-innovation: Implementing special education reform. *Harvard educational review,* 47:171–97.

Yudof, M. 1981. Legalization of dispute resolution, distrust of authority, and organizational theory. *Wisconsin law review* 1981:891–923.

DISPUTE RESOLUTION
IN EDUCATION:
AN INTRODUCTION TO
LITIGATION ALTERNATIVES

Steven S. Goldberg

Civil rights in the schools have for decades been developed and defined by litigation. In many areas, including desegregation, rights of disabled students, freedom of speech and conduct, and privacy of records, school officials have denied rights and then been ordered by courts to change their policies. The emerging area of dispute resolution, which includes negotiation and mediation, may be a useful adjunct to litigation that may reduce the financial and emotional transaction costs of the adversarial process. This chapter will describe the various elements of dispute resolution (sometimes called "alternative dispute resolution" or "ADR") and suggests that techniques such as negotiation and mediation may be useful ways to resolve conflict that arises in the schools (Goldberg & Lynch, 1992).

RECONSIDERING LITIGATION

The intensity and costs of disputing are so great—especially given limited resources for educational programs—that it is best to resolve conflict in a nonadversarial, nonlitigious manner. Obviously, helping children and treating staff fairly is a more constructive use of emotional capital for administrators than preparing for and worrying about litigation. Moreover, litigators have long assumed that the lawsuit was the best method for resolving disputes. That is the way that lawyers are socialized—to resolve conflict through law. Indeed, when Congress developed the most prescriptive dispute resolution procedure in education—the special education "due process" administrative hearing—the statute was based on the long-held assumption that the adversarial system is the best and fairest way to resolve disputes. It may not be, however, in the case of education (Goldberg & Kuriloff, 1991)

Litigation as a primary resort is being reconsidered. Law schools are beginning to incorporate training in negotiation and alternative dispute resolution ("ADR") into their curricula. A New York nonprofit organization, the Center for Public Resources, has for several years called upon corporate executives to adopt ADR procedures prior to using litigation. The benefit is twofold: first, it does away with the need for macho posturing by allowing these powerful CEO's the excuse that they are required to seek ADR as a consequence of the agreement. Second, it really may help to avoid quite costly litigation and to save time (CPR, 1989).

Another reason for implementing ADR, particularly in the schools in the era of restructuring, is that new relationships relating to power are now being considered. All members of the education community need to learn negotiation and dispute resolution techniques in order to get on with the business of education. Should we empower students? By allowing them access to ADR to resolve their concerns and to ameliorate discipline problems, they are given power in the school organization. According to Sarason (1990), a psychologist who has studied school culture, unless schools confront the obstacles—the power issues—that prevent reform, the reforms of the last several years will fail. If members of the school community feel they have no say, it is obvious they will resist change. One way to empower teachers and students is to allow them to negotiate and mediate disputes that formerly would have resulted in discipline for students and hard feelings for faculty members.

ADR has been used for centuries. A historian, Jerold Auerbach, in his book *Justice Without Law* (1983), documents mediation in a number of American communities. For example, mediation was used in religious communities in New England, in the seventeenth century. Now, people are using ADR for a variety of reasons. Since the 1960s, there has been a breakdown, perhaps, of traditional bonds that precluded conflict. People who move a good deal or who don't go to church with the same people they have known for years may prefer a somewhat more formal dispute resolution technique—rather than just sitting down with a neighbor and resolving a problem in an atmosphere of trust.

Judicial congestion has led to claims that justice is being denied and a feeling of disillusionment with courts, a sense that they not only take too long to respond, but they are also political or do not understand everyday problems. In addition, there is the obvious and longstanding distrust of attorneys. As a result, we saw in the 1980s an effort to define new ways of dispute resolution (Murray, Rau & Sherman, 1989). Who should use alternatives? Under what conditions?

Additional interest in ADR came as a result of various federal statutes. Foundations became active in this area. The Ford Foundation founded the National Center for Dispute Settlement and eventually the National Institute for Dispute Resolution or NIDR. The Neighborhood Justice Center was established in Atlanta; its special-education mediation model has been used in a number of states. The American Bar Association now has a Section on Dispute Resolution. Harvard Law School, Ohio State Law School, and Northwestern University have centers for the study and practice of ADR; Harvard's is responsible for the negotiation best seller, *Getting to Yes* (Fisher & Ury, 1991).

ALTERNATIVE DISPUTE RESOLUTION

According to Goldberg, Sander, and Rogers (1992) goals of dispute resolution techniques include the following: to lessen court congestion and to lessen the delay and costs involved in going to court; to enhance community involvement; to facilitate access to justice; and to provide more effective dispute resolution.

Forms of Dispute Resolution

There are several forms of ADR that could be applied to education disputes. The least intrusive is bargaining or negotiation. People get together and they try to work something out. The advantage of this method is that the parties involved have total control of the situation. For this reason, I always tell my clients in education matters that they should avoid the adversarial system if possible. Once they get into the system, they cannot predict what will happen. They should try to work things out. Lawyers and hearings and others dilute their control of their situation.

If parties are unable to settle a dispute themselves, they can bring in a third party who is neutral. This is known as mediation if the third party is there to assist the disputants to arrive at their own solution. If the third party imposes a solution, the process is known as adjudication. In a labor situation, this is usually called arbitration, which is binding or not, depending on the agreement of the parties. There is a continuum of "intrusiveness." The third party may be what is known as a "rent-a-judge." Or the process may be med-arb—if mediation does not work, arbitration will be tried. In some cases, the mediator switches hats and becomes an arbitrator. In others, a new person is brought in as an arbitrator.

Another hybrid process involves a mediator/investigator, the ombudsman (increasingly called the ombudsperson). We are all familiar with this concept. In America, this person usually works for the organization one is complaining about. For example, the *Washington Post* has an ombudsman who resolves questions from citizens who complain about issues that are reported in the newspaper. In Scandinavia, usually this person acts as an intermediary between the government and private citizens. In another hybrid alternative, a quick, or "summary," jury trial is attempted. Jurors chosen from a normal jury pool listen to evidence and give their opinion.

What are the factors for selecting the best dispute resolution method? There is no one best method but there are certain variables to take into account when thinking about ADR. First, what is the relationship among the parties? Is this a one-shot matter, or do they have a continuing relationship? In schools, that relationship lasts for perhaps eighteen years or more, depending on the number of children in one family who may attend school in the same community. If there is an ongoing relationship, it is important to work out problems in a way that will build relationships. Thus, negotiation or mediation would appear to be the method of choice.

One advantage of mediation is that it encourages a restructuring of the underlying relationship in a way that will mitigate conflict. An attorney may be able to resolve a dispute with litigation, but if it is possible to change the way parents and school officials interact, that is the most helpful way to go in the long run. "Did you ask the principal?" is always one of my first questions. "If not, go back and ask."

Another factor to consider is the nature of the dispute. Lon Fuller said that an adjudication is not well suited to an "allocational" dispute where there are no clear guidelines for a decision and where any solution has many ramifications. Fuller gives the example of a bequest of art to several museums. An adjudication may not be the best solution. One institution may really be a better place for a picture; for it, adjudication may not meet the desires of the claimants. Perhaps art experts can figure out what to do with the artwork.

Another factor is the frequency of the problem. Is the issue a recurring one or is it novel? In a novel dispute, such as a civil rights matter, perhaps adjudication is best so that a precedent is set for a large number of persons or a public policy is established. Desegregation is an example. Class actions in special education are another. A mundane problem that recurs could perhaps best be handled through arbitration. But you do not really want to negotiate civil liberties on a case-by-case basis.

The amount at stake is generally thought to be significant in determining the appropriateness of a dispute-resolution procedure. This may be speculation; there may be no connection between the amount and the procedure used. But speed and cost is a central issue. Arbitration may be simpler and more efficient than full-blown litigation, for example.

Finally, and perhaps most importantly, is the power relationship of the parties involved. An adjudication may be preferable when there is a strong power imbalance. The court may equalize the imbalance, though in a situation where a parent has limited funds for representation, discovery, or expert witnesses, this may not be the case.

In a RAND Corporation study (Hill & Madey, 1982), social science researchers found that power was a critical factor for public interest lawyers who were threatening lawsuits. The opportunity to control the special education system through litigation would have precluded consideration of less intrusive methods of dispute resolution. Yet, the mere availability of lawsuits may resolve an issue.

Arbitration is used in consumer or commercial matters, labor disputes, and increasingly, in disputes over lawyers' fees. It can be binding or nonbinding at the discretion of the parties.

Mediation has been used for many years to help employers and employees to resolve contract problems. It is increasingly being incorporated into child-custody disputes so that parents do not have to go into court to resolve each problem that arises. Of course, it is used in the schools.

Med-arb is used to solve issues that remain unsolved through the use of mediation.

Mini-trial has resolved corporate disputes. Cases are presented to senior executives of both parties. The executives then try to negotiate a settlement. A neutral advisor can be used to give an opinion as to what the result would be if the dispute were litigated, which sometimes breaks a deadlock.

In the "rent-a-judge" model, Judicial Arbitration and Mediation Service, or J.A.M.S., and Judicate retain retired judges to resolve business disputes, generally in a day. Judge Wapner is another example of a rent-a-judge. The litigants who appear in his courtroom are real people who agree to abide by his decisions. Under California law, his decisions are then considered to be an adjudication.

Concerns about Dispute Resolution

Certain cautions and concerns arise under ADR (Goldberg, Sander & Rogers, 1992; Singer, 1990). If it works, why is it not used more frequently?

Should it be compulsory? There has long been talk about making mediation compulsory under 94–142. Of course, it would violate the statute for states to require mandatory mediation in 94–142 matters because this would preclude the right to go through the administrative procedure and then to court.

Is there a danger under ADR of concentrating on the procedures rather than on fairness—the reason for ADR in the first place? Is there a danger of creating an imbalance between rich and poor, if we require the poor to engage in a "second-rate" dispute resolution process? Would they be precluded from asserting their rights in court?

Is there a danger in mediation, with its emphasis on accommodation, that large-scale structural change in schools would be impeded? Should the practice of ADR in the schools be regulated? Is there a fear of over-bureaucratization if ADR is more commonplace?

How can mediators help?

Linda Singer suggests several ways that mediators can bring parties together:

1. by soothing ruffled feelings
2. by ensuring that all parties have a say
3. by distinguishing interests from positions (what do you really want vs. what do you need to tell the public)
4. by working with the parties to devise creative solutions to their needs
5. by earning enough of the parties' trust so that they will share confidential information that may move things toward a settlement
6. by ferrying selected information back and forth, while at the same time changing language from negative to positive to create a better climate
7. by serving as an "agent of reality"—helping the parties to be more realistic about getting to an agreement
8. by keeping the negotiations going
9. by acting as a scapegoat when things go wrong, which takes pressure off the parties.

Mediators do not make the decision for the parties. If this happens, it is not mediation. Mediators have to gain trust so that the parties will confide in them. In this way, the mediator may discover areas of agreement. Unfortunately, the term mediator has been used so loosely, that anyone who hears it can presume it has maintained its original meaning. In some situations, mediators may not be purely neutral in their negotiating. Henry Kissinger, for example, in his shuttle diplomacy, was clearly representing the interests of the United States, yet, the overriding interest of all parties was avoiding bloodshed.

Every mediation has a number of similar stages that parties go through to resolve a dispute:

1. Initial contact is made.
2. The mediator enters into the dispute and sets the ground rules regarding the process.
3. The mediator gathers information regarding the dispute and everyong agrees on an agenda.
4. The mediator creates options for settling the dispute.
5. The mediator evaluates options for a settlement and compares them with the parties' alternatives to settlement.
6. Full or partial agreement on the dispute is reached, an agreement is written, and a method for implementation and monitoring of the dispute is determined.

Once the mediator establishes ground rules, the role of the mediator shifts. No party is allowed to take over. Open-ended, nonjudgmental questions are asked. What happened? The mediator tries to build momentum toward settlement by building on areas of agreement.

Mediators can meet with the parties jointly or separately. Joint meetings have several purposes: to allow disputants to hear each other's views, to express anger within a controlled setting, to identify areas of agreement and disagreement, and to help disputants with continuing relationships to learn to communicate better. A parent-school official conflict is particularly applicable here. Mediators can also meet separately so that parties can speak freely to the mediator about their concerns and explore settlement possibilities. For example, when I represent a teenager and a parent, I insist on meeting with them separately. They frequently have differing desires. "Did you throw the nails at the teacher?" "I did it, but I'm not going to tell my mother about it."

What are the purported advantages of mediation? Mediation allows the interested parties themselves to craft the solution at hand since the thought is that people are more likely to comply if they have developed the agreement. In other words, disputants have ownership of the settlement. There is a disputant "education" component, so disputants are made aware of the underlying relationship problems they have to work on. Mediation also ensures some sort of continuity in the relationship. Even when a mediation is not entirely successful, at least the communications process may have been improved. Mediation may also generate cooperation.

There are also disadvantages, however; there is no certainty that after the hours of negotiation, there will be any agreement at all. The interested parties in a complicated education dispute may change. People leave and

and take other positions. Since the outcome of a mediation does not have to be "principled," that is, based on law, people may not choose to go along with it. The mediators have no power to force implementation. And because parties may be in an imbalanced relationship of power, this imbalance may be reflected in the solution. In the long run, nobody is accountable for the final result.

How can mediation be used in schools?

Mediation has been used in a number of programs, especially student-peer mediation (ABA, 1988). In Washington, D.C., the SHARP Program is modeled after SMART—School Mediators Alternative Resolution Team. That program trains a couple of dozen student mediators and some faculty. It resolves disputes that may otherwise end in violence or dropping out of school. Indeed, the original purpose of these programs was to prevent dropouts in five New York City high schools and a junior high. Mediation has cut down on the suspension rate.

In San Francisco, elementary school students are being trained as mediators. Singer reports that pupils age four to six are mediating playground disputes and lunch money extortion rings. One sixth grader who wears a jersey emblazoned "conflict resolver" said, "We learned what are gestures such as crossing arms in anger mean to other people. We make sure to let people resolve it for themselves so they don't get angry."

Participating in mediation gives students a chance to cool off and express their anger in a non-threatening manner before the problem escalates. These programs are developed and maintained through Bar Association projects, such as one run in Santa Monica for a number of years. The National Association for Mediation in Education serves as a clearinghouse for identifying these programs.

In addition to keeping students in school, these programs have made teachers feel better about the discipline process. Perhaps most important, the students who have become mediators have increased self-esteem and want to stay in school. They have some power and control. One boy said, "at home I don't argue with my family as much."

Of course, there is a problem among some administrators who refuse to cede control to students who may want to develop these projects. And student challenges to authority have made little progress in the courts. Courts are loathe to intervene in school disputes, so students who seek mediation programs when refused are in some difficulty if they seek ADR.

The largest use of mediation in the schools has been in the special education context—the subject of my own research over the past couple of years (Goldberg & Kuriloff, 1991; Goldberg, 1982). Federally mandated dispute-resolution procedures include the right of parents and school officials to engage in a formal hearing over any aspect of a child's education program, such as tutoring or related services, presence or absence of a resource room, diagnosis by the school of a child's disability, or exclusion of a special education child for disciplinary reasons (*Honig v. Doe*).

Disagreements over special education have a number of aspects that make it seemingly viable for mediation. Disputants have a continuing relationship, and these disputes leave room for creative solutions. Indeed, there may be an entire range of options that are "appropriate" for an individual child (Goldberg & Kuriloff, 1991).

In larger states, mediators are available who are knowledgeable about both special education and mediation techniques, and there are advocacy groups. Federal and state statutes have created these entitlements, which are well-known and consistently enforced. In addition, the due process hearing is an incredibly cumbersome alternative to mediation. Finally, there is a community of interests. Not all parents are irrational, and not all school administrators evil. They are, in general, interested in a child's welfare. Mediation in education can help parents to move toward an agreement, which is the purpose of mediation.

At the other extreme are due process hearings, which are adversarial in nature. They are so complex and time consuming that they usually require lawyers or specially trained advocates. They are becoming increasingly legalistic. In some states now, lawyers can be hearing officers, which flies in the face of the original purpose of hearing officers, who should be law-trained special education experts who know a child's problems and the suitable programs that are available.

Hearings are cumbersome, time-consuming, and expensive. A typical hearing can cost $2,000 or more for hearing officer fees, transcripts, the time of school officials, expert witnesses, and the like. A mediation can cost between $100 and $500 per day and reduce stress. The goal in mediation is to get a signed agreement after one day. A hearing can last for many days, and it can take weeks for a hearing officer to issue an opinion.

Of course, mediation can be concurrent with a request for a due process hearing. It would be a violation of the statute to require mediation since this would preclude the right to request immediately a hearing to resolve conflict.

What does research say about mediation?

Does mediation work (Kressell & Pruitt, 1989)? Most, if not all of claims made in support of mediation, remain speculative. Whether mediation "works" or not may depend on the situation to which it is applied.

Is there user satisfaction? Generally, there is high user satisfaction. The rates of compliance are also usually fairly high. McEwan and Maiman (1984), two noted researchers in this field, have studied compliance in small claims court, another form of "quick justice," and their findings may offer some insight to user satisfaction with mediation. Why is satisfaction and compliance with a judgment high in this case? It is a quick and efficient system that gives parties "their day in court." In addition, the stakes of the parties are not that great. This finding can be contrasted to criminal matters or—as my study of fairness and satisfaction of special education due process hearings seems to demonstrate—education matters where the stakes to the parties are relatively high. In high-stakes areas, satisfaction is more closely related to winning, rather than to merely having an opportunity to present one's case. There may be a lesson for mediation usage in this conclusion. Perhaps mediation may not work— however informal, speedy, and efficient the process—when a child's right to an education is at stake. In other words, the stakes and not the process may affect user satisfaction with the process and eventual sense of fairness.

Mediation is likely to trigger a set of psychological dynamics that will be constructive in the resolution of disputes, including the opportunity for the parties to gain emotional support from the mediator and to explore a range of interpersonal reasons for reaching an agreement.

Does mediation speed cases and reduce court backlog? Evidence shows that cases that are mediated reach settlement more quickly than comparable cases that follow the traditional adversarial approach. It is uncertain if the cost is reduced when mediated cases are compared to cases that are settled. But there is no strong data that mediation reduces court congestion—one of the major arguments for engaging in mediation. In fact, many people who have access to mediation—perhaps one-third to two-thirds of those offered mediation—refuse to engage in it. They want to litigate.

Does mediation improve the post dispute climate? Again, there is no great support that mediation improves the post-dispute climate—another major argument for engaging in ADR. In my mediation study, the responses of parties are mixed. Some like it; some do not. Some evidence from international disputes, divorce mediation, and community justice research shows that mediation is unable to alter dysfunctional patterns in relationships. In fact, in nonindustrial societies, an anthropologist of mediation, Sally Merry (1990) found that mediation is used for the express purpose of maintaining unequal relationships. Perhaps this may be applicable to contemporary education disputes. Parties may seek mediation thinking they have more knowledge of the mediator's style and better advice, hoping to maintain the status quo.

Under what conditions is mediation effective? Mediation is effective when there is a low or moderate level of conflict or a strong motivation to reach an agreement. Also, when there is a commitment to mediation it can be effective. Mediation may work when there are resources available to effect the settlement. For example, school districts should not promise extensive educational programs if it does not have the resources to comply with the mediated agreement. An absence of issues of "principle" that will cause parties to be inflexible also improves the chances of success. A number of my clients came into the office saying they wanted to take their cases "all the way to the Supreme Court." Some say "I'll never give in."

In my research on special education mediation in New Jersey (Goldberg & Kuriloff, in preparation), the answers to the questions are still out. What are the characteristics of a successful mediation? The questions we asked in a study of over eighteen months asked parties under what conditions would they use mediation. What are the elements of a case that stops at the mediation stage? What elements lead the case to a due process hearing? The responses of a survey of several hundred parties, follow-up interviews, and observations of the process are not yet fully analyzed, but the initial sense is that mediation does not provide any greater sense of satisfaction with the process or sense of fairness in treatment than do due process administrative hearings. What is already clear is that "successful" mediations—defined as those that lead to agreement and are not pursued further through the administrative procedure—do take less time and cost less money than litigation. In response to the question, "Would you go through the process again," one parent answered, "Yes, the agreement was reached without the time effort and trauma of a due process hearing." This is precisely what advocates of mediation expect. For example, in Singer and Nace's oft-cited 1982 study of mediation in California and Massachusetts, mediation was found to resolve between 40 and 80 percent of the conflicts brought to the process. So there is a large range here, and the evidence is anecdotal in nature. But there is not a lot of information about the continuing relationship issue, whether or not people felt fairly treated and if parties believe the child's educational needs were properly met.

But there may be a less favorable picture. In response to our open-ended questions, some preliminary evidence suggests that the emotional cost of mediation may be too high in the case of special education. The parties generally come to mediations quite angry with each other. School officials resent being treated as defendants in a legally oriented procedure. They resent having their professional judgment questioned. Parents resent not getting what they are seeking.

Even when they settle, parties often report that their relationships are unimproved. For example, the parent of one student said, "Our relationship has gotten worse," while a school official reported, "No change. The parents have always been suspicious of all our recommendations." Another school official replied, "The relationship with the parents has always been difficult, and it has remained so."

These findings may suggest that special education disputes may simply not be resolvable through mediation—or mediation is no greater help than any other method of dispute resolution. After all, the parents are involved in the most profound issues evoking the most basic protective instincts and the deepest identifications. By the time parents and schools are in serious disagreement, it is probably too late for anything but the adversarial process. If mediation proves to be a cheaper and less traumatic way for resolving even half of these disputes, it will prove its worth. On a broader level, the only real solution may lie in prevention.

If schools can come to understand the complex psychological issues they must encounter whenever they deal with a parent of a handicapped child—or when they decide a previously "normal" child is "handicapped"—they may start to develop imaginative approaches to collaborating with parents from the beginning. Only approaches such as those are likely to prevent the emotionally and economically draining battles that occur when schools and parents come to disagree about what is in the best educational interests of the child.

REFERENCES

American Bar Association. 1988. *Education and mediation: Explaining the alternatives.* Chicago: Author.

Auerbach, J. 1983. *Justice without law?* Oxford: Oxford University Press.

Center for Public Resources. 1989. *CPR practice guide.* New York: Author.

Fisher, R., and W. Ury. 1991. *Getting to yes,* 2d ed. Boston: Houghton, Mifflin.

Goldberg, S. S. 1982. *Special education law: A guide for parents, advocates, and educators.* New York: Plenum.

————. and P. Kuriloff. 1991. Evaluating the fairness of special education hearings. *Exceptional children.* 57:546–55.

————. (in preparation). *Special education mediation in New Jersey.*

Goldberg, S. B., F. Sander, and N. Rogers. 1992. *Dispute resolution,* 2d ed. Boston: Little, Brown.

Hill, P., and D. Madey. 1982. *Educational policy making through the civil justice system.* Santa Monica, CA: Rand.

Kressel, K., and D. G. Pruitt. 1989. *Mediation research: The process and effectiveness of third-party intervention.* San Francisco: Jossey-Bass.

Merry, S. 1990. *Getting justice and getting even.* Chicago: University of Chicago Press.

Murray, J., A. Rau, and E. Sherman. 1989. *Process of dispute resolution: The role of lawyers.* Westbury, New York: Foundation Press.

Sarason, S. B. 1990. *The predictable failure of educational reform: Can we change course before it's too late?* San Francisco: Jossey-Bass.

Singer, L. R. 1990. *Settling disputes* Boulder, CO: Westview.

————, and E. Nace. 1982. *Mediation in special education.* Washington, D.C.: National Institute for Dispute Resolution.